Rolf Boldrewood

ROLF BOLDREWOOD is known mainly for one book, *Robbery Under Arms*, but Thomas Alexander Browne, who chose that name as his pseudonym, wrote a great deal more—sixteen other novels, two novelettes, a couple of handbooks on farming, two volumes of essays and stories, and several uncollected articles. For a part-time author whose first piece was accepted when he was forty years old, he achieved much. His first novel appeared as a serial in 1873 and his last in 1905: he was then seventy-nine, and still had ten years to live. In all his writing, as in his life, he promoted ideals of hard work, honesty, education and a belief in good breeding that would have come more naturally from an English lord than from the son of a sea captain.

His father, Sylvester John Brown (the family added the final 'e' between 1862 and 1866) had been an officer with the East India Company, and after visiting Sydney in 1820 had decided to return to live there. He sailed with cargo in the West Indies, but it was on his own ship that he met his future wife, Eliza Alexander, while she was travelling as a passenger to Mauritius. They lived in London after their marriage and it was there that Thomas was born on 6 August 1826, the eldest of ten children, only one of whom died in infancy. Sylvester, an energetic adventurer, captained his own barque, the *Proteus*, from Plymouth to Hobart Town in 1831, sailing on 14 April and landing his cargo of 112 convicts on 3 August. The *Proteus* arrived in Sydney on 28 August and Sylvester settled with his wife and three children in fashionable Spring Street. For about four years he engaged in whaling, giving it up to build a country house he called Enmore three miles from town, where it eventually gave its name to a Sydney suburb. It was an impressive stone mansion with a veranda twelve feet wide around it, an idea garnered from Sylvester's Indian visits. Young Tom attended Sydney College, at first walking but later riding on a Timor pony. His education had begun at a dame school in O'Connell Street and then continued at William Cape's Sydney Academy in King Street. When Cape became headmaster of Sydney College on its foundation in 1835—it was later to become Sydney Grammar School—he transferred his pupils there; at the first examinations Thomas Alexander was awarded a prize of books for Latin. His schoolmates included future premiers in James Martin and John Robertson, as well as many others who were to become famous in Australian history. In his sixties Browne wrote with affection of 'My School Days' and 'Sydney Fifty Years Ago'.

His restless father, attracted by the new country to the south, overlanded stock to Mount Alexander in 1838, returning later to take his family to Port Phillip by ship. It could not have been easy for Eliza to exchange the spacious comfort of Enmore for the wattle and daub of the new settlement. Tom went back to Sydney for about two years as a boarder at Sydney College and then finished his schooling under the Reverend David Boyd, previously a Classics master at Sydney College but by then also living in Melbourne. Browne always advocated the need for a sound, classically based education and most of his heroes are successful at least partly because they have had one. The ebullient Sylvester busied himself in many areas. He began a ferry service between Melbourne and Williamstown with the first steamer to sail on Port Phillip Bay, the *Firefly*. He bought a cattle run of 2,000 acres at Darebin Creek; took up land for farming near Mount Macedon; bought allotments in Flinders, Collins and Elizabeth Streets, seventy acres of the Toorak subdivision and 320 acres at Heidelberg, where he built a comfortable house he named Hartlands. By that time Tom was thirteen years old and had five sisters; in 1843 he came home from school, as he says, 'for good'. The family were part of the 'more or less aristocratic section of the community',[1] but the depression which had begun in 1841 ruined Sylvester and almost certainly led to his physical and nervous collapse about five years later. Young Tom decided to recoup the family fortunes and in 1843 he set out for the western district of Victoria, making a 200-mile journey with a family friend, the Reverend John Bolden, who was visiting a property near the old whaling station of Port Fairy. The area impressed Tom so much that in the next year at the age of seventeen he took up a run of about 32,000 acres in this rich district (although in his reminiscences of this event he speaks of about 50,000 acres). Part of the run was marshland, through which flowed the Eumeralla River, and as a self-described 'devout worshipper' of Sir Walter Scott Tom named his holding Squattlesea Mere after Sir Roger Wildrake's home in *Woodstock*.[2] In the essays written during the seventies and published as *Old Melbourne Memories* in 1884, Browne described how he and his folk—Old Tom, 'my venerable guide and explorer' (p. 33), Mr Cunningham, an experienced bushman, and a married couple, Joe Burge and his wife—lived first under the dray,

4

Melbourne

OXFORD UNIVERSITY PRESS

LONDON WELLINGTON NEW YORK

Oxford University Press, Ely House, London, W.1

GLASGOW NEW YORK TORONTO MELBOURNE WELLINGTON
CAPE TOWN IBADAN NAIROBI DAR ES SALAAM LUSAKA ADDIS ABABA
DELHI BOMBAY CALCUTTA MADRAS KARACHI LAHORE DACCA
KUALA LUMPUR SINGAPORE HONG KONG TOKYO

Oxford University Press, 7 Bowen Crescent, Melbourne

© *Alan Brissenden 1972*

First published 1972

ISBN 0 19 550404 6

Registered in Australia for transmission by post as a book
PRINTED BY JOHN SANDS PTY. LTD. HALSTEAD PRESS DIVISION

then in a sod hut and finally in a 'real mansion' (p. 38), a three-roomed hut of split slabs.

Despite his declaration of pride at having 'My run! My own station!' (p. 35) Browne did not hold the licence himself. This was made out to William Walker, a merchant and investor who had married Browne's eldest sister some time before 1846. The licence was later transferred to Tom who held it from 1851 to 1862. The romantic fiction that he had been a landowner for more than those years was to become indispensable to him in his later life.

On Sylvester's breakdown in 1846, loss of his properties, and mortgage foreclosures, Mrs Browne, the children, and their old nurse, who had the splendid name of Annie Roebuck, came to the run; there were by then ten in the family altogether. It is not clear what became of Sylvester between that time and his death in about 1861. Fires had burnt out the country and while Tom's mother complained, 'I thought you told me this was a rich country; I call it a howling desert', Tom himself gloried in his position, and later remarked, 'I was the eldest son, appointed ruler and director of the family fortunes and henceforth with unquestionable powers and privileges'.[3] It was characteristic that in the reversal of circumstances he expressed no bitterness.

He stayed at Squattlesea Mere for about fifteen years, and his reminiscences recall kangaroo hunts, evenings at neighbouring stations, often browsing in well-stocked libraries, dances, race meetings, balls and picnics as well as the hard work of pioneering life. His descriptions of 'those good old days' in the western district and the settlers there, many of them Scots, are nostalgic recollections of friendships and the pastoral life; chronologically they are occasionally inaccurate but they provide, nevertheless, an interesting pattern of social detail. Browne's experiences during those years formed a basis for much of his writing, and they remained with him. As late as 1908 he was remembering in a letter to Evan Hunter, whose uncle had settled near Mount Gambier in the fifties, that 'my sister Eliza . . . was a great friend of your Uncle Frank, and had many a dance with him in the old Port Fairy days when balls were frequent and the "Mount Gambier Mob" thought nothing of riding to our race meetings'[4]—even though it was a distance of over a hundred miles.

The Aboriginals were troublesome and Browne's kindliness is shown in his unfashionably sympathetic attitude to them. He was advised to keep the blacks away from the station but at first he adopted instead a policy of conciliation, believing 'it was their country, after all'.[5] When his own house was pillaged, however, and his cattle stolen and speared he realized that he and the few other like-minded squatters in the district could not avoid the assaults and reprisals that took place. Although in his earlier writing his attitude to the Aboriginals is tolerant and constructive, in 1906 he wrote a severe attack against treating them leniently, saying at one point, 'under an apparently peaceable, even grateful demeanour, lurks at all times an untrustworthy, treacherous disposition, ready at all times to assert itself in acts of violence, when actuated by greed or fancied unfairness';[6] and this attitude is given expression in the character of Warrigal in *Robbery Under Arms*.

Squattlesea Mere prospered, particularly with cattle and horse breeding and, later, potato growing. Browne's care and enthusiasm for horses, which lasted all his life, matured during this period, when he broke and trained several himself. A number of his shorter essays and stories are about horses, and in 'The Horse You Don't See Now' he writes warmly about his two favourite harness horses. There is no indication whether he used to lay bets, and it is unlikely in view of the strict attitude to gambling he takes in, for example, *Babes in the Bush*; but into his old age he kept newspaper cuttings about horses and horse racing.

In 1858 the family was able to return to Hartlands, their Heidelberg property, and to become the 'social Brownes' once more, then two years later Thomas Alexander took a trip to England, Ireland and Scotland which provided the basis for his serial 'Incidents and Adventures of My Run Home' (1874). On this visit he stayed in various parts of England and with relatives in Ireland, enjoying the hunting, racing and society life. After returning to Australia in February 1861 he was married on 1 August to Margaret Maria Riley of Raby, between Liverpool and Camden. As Margaret's grandfather, Alexander Riley, had introduced Saxon merino sheep into Australia, Browne was marrying into a family important to the pastoral industry.

Like his father before him, he was attracted by new ventures, and he sold his Squattlesea Mere cattle run to buy Murrabit, a sheep station on Lake Boga near Swan Hill; the records show that the licence was transferred in February 1862, though Browne himself says that he went there in 1858. Whenever the change was made it was a grimly unfortunate one. Good seasons were followed by bad and it appears that the purchaser of Squattlesea Mere could not keep up his repayments; as a result Browne was forced to sell Murrabit in 1863. In the following year he took up Bundidgaree, a sheep station of 28,160 acres near Narrandera on the Murrumbidgee, and stayed there until drought finally drove him off the land in 1869. The lease of this station was in the names of two of his brothers-in-law, Robert Massie and Molesworth Greene, and it is possible that he was the manager for them rather than the owner, as he always presents himself. Alternatively, as T. Inglis Moore has suggested, the arrangement may have been like a mortgage with Massie and Greene holding the lease as security.[7] If so, then Browne resembled his ideal, Scott, closely in that he wrote to pay off his debts, though probably there would have been no need for this until 1870, when he moved to the Sydney suburb of Ashfield with his wife and family, by that time two girls and two boys. Twins were born while the Brownes were living there and it was then that Tom began writing for money. His first essay to be printed had been an account of a kangaroo hunt, written in 1865 when he was laid up with a bruised ankle, the result of a horse kick. He had sent it to the *Cornhill Magazine*, who published it in 1866; another, an account of shearing in the Riverina, was accepted by the same journal in 1868. These were written mainly to pass the time but the need for extra money now led him to use his pen with a purpose and, when the editor of the newly established *Town and Country Journal* accepted some short pieces on pastoral life, Tom found he could add £150 a year to his income. In the issue for 22 October 1870, for instance, his 'Shearing in the Riverina' appeared under his first pseudonym, 'Templar', an appropriate name for an admirer of Sir Walter's romances. Although he nowhere directly records any despondency, leaving the land after twenty-five years must have been a disheartening blow to Browne especially as, with melodramatic irony, the drought broke in 1870 and ushered in several good seasons.

He had been helped previously by three of his brothers-in-law, first Walker and then Greene and Massie. He was now helped by a fourth, Frederick Darley, a successful Sydney barrister married to his sister Eliza. Darley was to become Chief Justice in 1886; he was knighted in 1887 and appointed Lieutenant-Governor in 1891. Browne had been a Justice of the Peace while at Bundidgaree and had acted as Chairman of the Narrandera Bench in the absence of the Police Magistrate. (He later used his judicial experiences as short story material; one of his most interesting cases, for instance, was the murder of the Poulman brothers, two German hawkers whose bodies were burned after they were killed—an incident which was the basis for 'The Mailman's Yarn' in the collection *In Bad Company* of 1901.) Through Darley's influence, in April 1871 he was appointed Police

Magistrate at Gulgong, at that time the fastest growing gold-mining town in New South Wales: between 1871 and 1873 the population swelled from 4,000 to 30,000. He was formally appointed Goldfields Commissioner in 1872, and then District Coroner. Browne's yearly salary was £428, but if, as seems probable, Darley had paid off his immediate debts and was taking half this in return, the income from his writing was now not only useful but virtually essential.

His inexperience as a public servant was not lost on the townspeople, and one of the newspapers, the *Gulgong Guardian*, gave him a distinctly unencouraging welcome:

> While admitting in every way Mr Browne's qualifications for his manifold duties, we think that a frontage gold field like Gulgong, should have been favoured with the appointment of an experienced officer to rule over the destinies of the miners, as no matter how apt and energetic an inexperienced man may be in learning his Gold Commissioner's duty, he cannot give that satisfaction so necessary to repress the litigation that rapidly springs up when the regulations are not firmly administered. We feel sure that Mr Browne will endeavour to act justly, but man—especially in gold-mining—is so prone to err.

Browne mastered the difficult and various roles he had undertaken and became respected as a benevolent but firm magistrate. He was active in many ways as a leader in the community. He organized the building of the local Church of England, led a committee which established a School of Arts library, chaired another which had a hospital erected, presided over social occasions like the luncheon for Anthony Trollope in October 1871, and attended dinners for celebrities like the Chief Justice.

Some people, indeed, felt that he was neglecting his duties and in 1873 he was attacked by the editor of the *Guardian*, F. de Courcey Browne, who wrote, 'defective as he is as a Commissioner, he is worse as a Justice', and complained of 'the slovenly, muddling method of management as carried out on this goldfield'. Soon after, a letter insulting to Browne was published by the *Guardian*, and de Courcey Browne was tried for libel in Sydney, where he was given a six months gaol sentence. The Goldfields Commissioner, however, successfully petitioned the court to reduce the sentence and even the *Guardian* was moved 'to acknowledge the lenient view taken of this case by Mr Commissioner Browne, than whom no one had greater reason to be offended'.[8] From remarks made in the *Gulgong Mercantile Advertiser* for 13 March 1873 it is clear that de

Courcey Browne had applied unsuccessfully for the position of Goldfields Commissioner; his attacks were thus basically personal. In June 1873 he appeared before the Magistrate on a charge of larceny, and was sent for trial—an ironic conclusion to the relationship between the pugnacious newspaper editor and his namesake on the Bench.

Browne's public life involved him in much effort for the community at Gulgong, and Keast Burke[9] suggests that his life in Gulgong was far from happy, as he was continually being accused of misunderstanding the miners and failing to appreciate their problems. While this is true of the first few years, the gold fever died down in the late seventies, the population fell and the strain must have accordingly lessened. As well, the appointment in 1874 of the first Under Secretary for the New South Wales Department of Mines would have relieved him, and other hard-pressed commissioners, of much on-the-spot responsibility.

He was able to retain something of his pastoral existence by settling with his family outside the busy gold-rush atmosphere of the town at Guntawang, a squatter's homestead about five miles from Gulgong; he drove in each morning. It was his practice always to rise early, about five or six, and write for an hour or two before breakfast. By the time he was established on the goldfields he was writing regularly, and with some success. During his mornings at Guntawang he relived his early experiences for the *Town and Country Journal*, the weekly paper which had begun to accept short articles from him in 1870. His first serial was 'The Fencing of Wanderowna', a piece of propaganda for fencing sheep runs which would have been out of date even in 1873 when it appeared; this backward-looking attitude is an interesting indication of Browne's personality, general philosophy and literary outlook—throughout his writing career he drew on the past and especially on his own life. Drought, floods, fire and the suicide of an old shepherd are among the tribulations which beset the young heroes, Gilbert and Hobbie Elliott. Like the majority of Browne's stories, it has a clear moral purpose. Because they fence their run, the Elliotts become successful squatters, the goal of many of his heroes. This was the first of eleven serials that Browne wrote. Ten were later published as novels—'The Wild Australian' is the only exception—and of these all but one, *Ups and Downs*, appeared after the heartening success of *Robbery Under Arms* in 1888.

The article 'How I Began to Write' contains a clear account

9

of his methods, very different in their reliability from those of Dickens, or Marcus Clarke:

> The method of composition which I employed, though regular, was not fatiguing, and suited a somewhat desultory turn of mind. I arranged for a serial tale by sending the first two or three chapters to the editor, and mentioning that it would last a twelvemonth, more or less. If accepted, the matter was settled. I had but to post the weekly packet, and my mind was at ease. I was rarely more than one or two chapters ahead of the printer; yet in twenty years I was only once late with my instalment, which had to go by sea from another colony. Every author has his own way of writing; this was mine.[10]

His daughter Emily told a correspondent that when he was travelling on circuit he used to write in inns, living rooms and more or less wherever he could. As well as using the early mornings he would also write after dinner until bedtime and claimed to have done five or six hours of writing a day in this way.[11] The steady progression of his composition is reflected in the stories themselves; most are straightforward tales uncomplicated by much intrigue of plot or development of character.

His second serial, 'Incidents and Adventures of My Run Home' (1874), gave him the opportunity to indulge his romantic imagination; it also showed his inability with emotional dialogue. All but one of the next four serials were concerned with pastoral life, 'The Squatter's Dream' of 1875 being especially autobiographical, for the hero, Jack Redgrave, sells his cattle run, Marshmead, has adventures with floods, bushrangers, Aboriginals and dishonest businessmen, and sinks to becoming a shepherd and finally a stable help in an inn. Though Browne did not reach this level, he did go droving in 1870. He, of course, did sell Squattlesea Mere while his hero, Jack Redgrave, awakens to find himself still at Marshmead, the advertisement he has written for the sale of his run lying unposted on the table before him. Or so it was in the serial. In 1878 the story was published, his first book, by the London firm of colonial suppliers and outfitters, S. W. Silver & Co. They altered the name to *Ups and Downs* and concocted a new ending in which Jack recouped his fortunes by taking up another run. In this changed form the book was republished by Macmillan in 1890 and thereafter; the original title was used again, even though the whole disastrous line of events was no longer merely a dream. It was probably the realistic aspects of the story which led Silver & Co. to make it the first, and apparently only, book in a series, 'Readings for Colonists', and, more importantly, to commission from Browne two books each with the title of *S. W. Silver & Co.'s Australian Grazier's Guide*, one on sheep farming, which appeared in 1879, the second, on cattle raising, in 1881. These are uncomplicated, helpful manuals touched occasionally with the romanticism of his fiction. The successful cattle breeder, for instance, returns to live in England 'upon a fine estate purchased with the proceeds of Australian pastoral enterprise' (p. 120). Browne, hardpressed Police Magistrate and Goldfields Commissioner, wrote even in a handbook of his own dream, now that it was past fulfilment. The *Grazier's Guides* were published anonymously and never publicly acknowledged by their author, who had no need to be ashamed of them.

By now Browne could have begun considering himself a reasonably successful writer, but his greatest triumph was to come. In 1881 he left Gulgong, which had declined to a town of less than 5,000, and was appointed Police Magistrate at Dubbo, a rural centre on the Macquarie River in the central west of New South Wales. It was here that he began *Robbery Under Arms* early one morning in February 1882, two years after a friend had suggested he write a bushranger novel. He sent the first two chapters off to the *Australasian*, which had been publishing some of his pastoral sketches; its rejection was a shock to the author, who then sent it to the *Town and Country Journal*; astonishingly, it was refused again, and Browne tried the *Sydney Mail*, which had not published him before. Here it was accepted, and the publication began on 1 July of a story which has become a classic of Australian adventure fiction.[12]

As Rolf Boldrewood, Browne was now a fairly well-known author in Australia, and when he was moved from Dubbo to Armidale as Police Magistrate in 1884 he was cordially welcomed by the local press. The records show that he was humanitarian and just on the bench, and particularly severe on drunkenness when it caused hardship to families.[13] *Old Melbourne Memories*, his only book to be first published in Australia, appeared in that year. Despite the title, the essays in this collection are mainly about events and personalities of the Port Fairy days; they were first printed in the *Australasian*. The New England climate was too cold and damp for Mrs Browne and their three sons and five daughters and in the following year they moved south to Albury on the Murray River where Tom, now fifty-eight, was appointed Chairman of the Land Licensing Board. In 1887 he was appointed a Police Magistrate and Mining Warden again, adding usefully to his income, and he remained at Albury until his retirement in 1895. During those years nine of his stories appeared in hard covers, all but one of them (*A Modern Buc-caneer*) having been serialized before, as well as the previously unpublished novelette, *The Sphinx of Eaglehawk*, which had a goldfield setting. The flood began with *Robbery Under Arms*, which was published in London with some alterations and excisions in 1888 by Remington and Company. Soon after, Remington sold the rights for £50 to Macmillan who reprinted it twice in 1889, four times in 1890, three times in 1891 and at least twenty-five times more over the next fifty years; several other editions also appeared during that period and it has continued in print ever since. It is an attractive irony that this upright magistrate should have paid off his debt to a Chief Justice with the rewards from a bushranging story.

The great popularity of *Robbery Under Arms* led Macmillan to publish almost everything else that Browne had written for magazines. They had discovered another author to set beside Kipling, F. Marion Crawford, Mrs Humphry Ward and other popular writers of 'Macmillan's Colonial Library of copyright books for circulation only in India and the Colonies'. Now they would even publish *The Squatter's Dream*, which they had refused when Frederick Darley had offered it on a visit to England in 1876. Events were gathering speed too quickly for Browne, who protested that he wanted to restore and revise the book after its mutilation by Silver & Co.'s reader; he felt it contained some of his best work. After this first protest, however, he did not complain. The sudden shower of royalties would have silenced any but the most querulous of authors. His initial terms for *Robbery Under Arms* were one-sixth after the first 200 of the English edition were sold, and 6d on the colonial edition. By 1893 he was being offered £250 in advance for a book, one-fifth on a three-volume edition, one-sixth on a one-volume edition and 6d on the colonial edition.

When he retired from the public service in June 1895 Browne entered Melbourne society as a successful author, well known abroad as well as at home. A member of the Melbourne Club since 1854, he now used it as his address, and was especially tickled when he received letters sent there to 'Rolf Boldrewood'. Comfortably off, if not rich, in excellent health, as he always was until a year before his death, Browne enjoyed his later years as fully as he had his earlier life as a squatter. A well built man of middle height, genial and kindly, he had an even, regular existence. In his seventy-eighth year he wrote, 'It is a queer feeling to have most of the feelings of middle age and yet to be nearer *eighty* years of age than the allotted term of threescore years and ten'.[14] He kept a daily journal, and a few have survived from this period of his retirement. They mainly record the state of the weather, national events and domestic affairs, and contain little of the introspection or reflection that can illuminate for the biographer the diarist's life and time. He enjoyed his success, believed that his writing was good, and had small regard for adverse critics; 'it is not worthwhile troubling one's head about the average critic', he wrote to his publisher in 1895. 'He is only accidentally right as a rule. The public which reads and buys what it finds interesting is the chief and "predominant" reviewer. I claim to know what I write about . . .'[15] He notes frequently in his diaries that he is correcting and re-reading but in fact he did almost no revising or cutting of the serials that were now appearing in hard covers. He spent a great deal of time at the Club, doing much of his writing there, and it is an indication of the esteem in which he was held that he is one of only three members who were not presidents whose portraits hang there. Horses continued to be an interest with him, and the Melbourne Cup was 'the Great Event of the Year'. His excellent health allowed him to go dancing—he went to two balls and a garden party at Government House in 1898, for example, and in his seventy-eighth year he was still enjoying the Lancers, and getting home at 2.30 a.m. His 'dear wife' was an excellent gardener and published an informative book, *The Flower Garden in Australia*, in 1893. She later had a long illness, however, and the eldest daughter, Rose, was a frequent social companion for Browne.

A lovable and loving family man, he kept in close contact with his brothers and sisters, visiting Emma, Mrs Molesworth Greene, and her family at Bacchus Marsh, for instance, on several happy occasions. In 1904, when she was seventy-five, he was distressed to find her decaying into senility. 'Why this disintegration of mind —of mental harmony, should have taken place', he wrote in his diary, 'is hard to account for. She is a very clever, well educated woman—strong in mind and once strong in body'.[16] A comment like this indicates a limitation of his understanding which reduces the range and depth of Browne's novels, especially so far as characterization is concerned. He rarely touches on human suffering, and then only briefly, as in the imprisonment of Lance Trevanion in the hulks in *Nevermore*, or in a sentimentalized fashion, as in *The Sealskin Cloak*. Yet he was familiar with illness through his own family, and he had seen plenty of cases of hardship on the goldfields.

His sons and daughters and their children were a delight to

him, and in some measure the boys lived out his own hopes for himself; his eldest son, Everard, went on the land, and Browne stayed at his property Cororooke, near Colac, in western Victoria; Gerald became a mining engineer, and young Tom went gold-mining in Western Australia. Four of his five daughters married, and the families visited each other a good deal during the 1890s. Rose, who remained unmarried, had some literary ability; she published a novel, *The Complications at Collaroi*, in 1911, using the pseudonym 'Rose Boldrewood', and between 1922 and 1929 was connected with a series of articles about her father in the *Australasian*, the *Sydney Mail* and the *Queenslander*. He died aged eighty-nine on 11 March 1915 after a year's illness and was buried in Brighton Cemetery, not far from the grave of Adam Lindsay Gordon.

Robbery Under Arms was, and still is, frequently linked by commentators with *For the Term of his Natural Life* and *Geoffry Hamlyn*. Browne admired Clarke, acknowledged a debt to Kingsley, and revered Shakespeare. In Melbourne he took part in regular monthly Shakespearean play readings, with a group of friends which included the historian George Rusden. But his devotion to the prose and verse of Scott, 'the Magician' as he called him, was life-long. At eighty-three he wrote that he had begun to read him when he was six or seven and still did. References to Scott occur frequently in all his writing, the most bizarre in *The Miner's Right*, where a new chum discovers an Aboriginal wrapped in a blanket under a shady tree reading one of Sir Walter's novels (p. 356). He learns afterwards that the native, Bungaree, had been educated at an early age, and had then reverted to his bush ways without losing his European tastes. The most extensive use of Scott is in *The Last Chance* (1905), Browne's final novel, where the Bannerets, a colonial family who have bought an English estate, make a pilgrimage to Abbotsford, and as evening entertainment hold a 'Sir Walter Scott symposium' in which everyone must recite a favourite passage, either verse or prose. Scott's romanticism is the most obvious literary influence on Browne. Descriptions of mountain landscapes in *Nevermore* and *Babes in the Bush*, for example, could slip almost unnoticed into one of the highland novels. The stilted, melodramatic dialogue of Scott's worst passages, especially the passionate exchanges between lovers, is intensified in Browne, and his characterization of women is generally inept even when compared with a heroine so incredible as Diana Vernon of *Rob Roy*, let alone the impressive Helen McGregor from the same novel. The names of his own books and charac-

14

ters were of great importance to Browne, but the aristocratic titles of Scott's medieval nobility and their descendants sit incongruously on the children of the colonies. Names like Isora Delmar, Sir Tudor Walladmar, Bertram Devereux or Hypatia Tollemache are ill-sorted with the bush settings and realism of much of the action of Browne's writing.

Throughout his life he continued his habit of reading, but Scott was never supplanted as his favourite, and he read and reread him into his old age. Shakespeare, Kingsley, Clarke, Longfellow, Tennyson; these were his standbys. Dickens, Hardy, or the newer novelists like Bennett and Wells do not seem to have impinged on his taste, and the growing nationalism of Australian writing and the *Bulletin* attitude of radical patriotism were distasteful to him. He remarked on Victor Daley as a truly poetic new writer, but his romantic attitude led him to overenthusiastic judgement of his lesser contemporaries. In an address to the fourth meeting of the Australasian Association for the Advancement of Science at Hobart in January 1892, he fulsomely and indiscriminately praised the work of Wentworth, Kendall, Clarke, William Foster, Brunton Stephens and William Bede Dalley. Kingsley's *Geoffry Hamlyn*, however, he described as 'the first, the finest Australian work of fiction worthy of the subject, of the great, the heroic subject of Australasian Colonisation'.[17] Lady novelists are especially lauded— Tasma, 'the Australian "George Elliott" [sic]', Mrs Humphry Ward, Mrs Praed, Mona Caird and Mrs Martin, the writer of *An Australian Girl*. Browne's flowery rhetoric is in contrast to the quieter remarks of Alexander Sutherland, then acting as Professor of Literature at Melbourne University, who considered most of the writers mentioned by Browne as pioneers—for the more perceptive Sutherland the most important poet was Charles Harpur. This address was Browne's only extended piece of criticism. He also wrote brief forewords to four books, including a laudatory preface to Banjo Paterson's *Poems* (1895) and a review of *The Silence of Dean Maitland* for the *Sydney Quarterly Magazine*, which was more social than literary in content: it trenchantly attacks the misrepresentation of the native-born Australian, a theme he had already taken up in 'The Stage Australian' for the same journal.[18] While a devoted Anglophile, he continually asserted the equality of the Australian and the Englishman in everything but blood, not only in his novels but also in his shorter contributions to journals and newspapers. Several of these were collected in *Old Melbourne Memories* (1884), *A Romance of Canvas Town* (1898) and *In Bad Company*

15

(1901); the best are those written from his own experiences. He always refers to himself as Rolf Boldrewood, even though others, the settlers in the Port Fairy district, for instance, are given their own names.

His belief in what he considered to be literary language often leads to flabbiness in his writing because several words are used where one would do: grass is 'thick-growing verdant sward', country girls are 'fair daughters of the land', birds are 'Dame Nature's feathered families' and so on. Least affected are his personal reminiscences about horses, which make up about a third of the *In Bad Company* pieces. Some of these have the direct appeal of good journalism, like this part of a description of Ben Bolt, from 'Old Time Thoroughbreds':

> Ben Bolt . . . was a bright chestnut, with four white legs, a broad blaze, and a considerable quantity of white in the corners of his eyes, with which he had an uncanny way of regarding his rider. He was truly illustrious in more ways than one. There is no record of any white man (or black one either) having seen him tired. At the end of the longest day, or the most terrific 'cutting-out' work, Ben's head was up, his clear eyes watchful, his uneasy tail, switching slowly from side to side, like a leopard not fully agitated. He had been known to leave Melbourne after a trip with fat cattle (his rider had a young wife on the station certainly), and late on the second day the marshes of the Eumeralla were in sight. A hundred and eighty miles—winter weather too! I can state from personal experience that as a hackney he was deliciously easy, fast and free. But the luxurious sensation of being so charmingly carried was modified by the ever-present thought that he could 'buck you into a tree-top' whenever it so pleased him; and at what minute the fit might take him no one had ever been able to foretell. (p. 382)

Here, the personal tone and unpretentious language are all that is required. The picture is sharply created, and the owner's affection is clearly expressed. He is writing mostly as he would speak, not in a self-consciously 'artistic' manner, but plainly and simply. The more factual sections of the novels, especially of *The Miner's Right* and *Robbery Under Arms*, are also distinguished by a closeness to the spoken word, although this had always been the better aspect of his style, especially when he was writing to give information, as in the *Grazier's Guides*.

During his last years a curious fiction arose that Browne's most successful novel was also his first; in 1912, for example, it was stated in an article in the *Bookman* that he had written only a few occasional sketches before *Robbery Under Arms*.[19] The truth, of course, was different. He had written well over

16

half of all his published work before 1888—ten novels, in serial form, the two handbooks for emigrants, and numerous short pieces, some of which had already been collected as *Old Melbourne Memories*. It is understandable that his family would want him to be remembered by his most famous book; what was not recognized at the time was that *Robbery Under Arms* stands outside the general body of his novels as a whole. As a bush-ranging tale narrated by a native-born Australian, it is distinct from the others, which fall conveniently, if loosely, into three groups—nine are romances or romantic adventures, six are mainly pastoral and one is a mining story.

The romances began with 'Incidents and Adventures of My Run Home' (1874), a fictionalized autobiography in which Browne first used the name 'Boldrewood', both for himself as narrator and for the ancestral home he visits, Boldrewood Chase. He took it from Scott's *Marmion*, and added 'Rolf' because he felt it had a good Norse ring to it. The story is a sequence of events rather than a novel, for there is little interplay of character. Already apparent, however, is a conflict in attitude which makes for a certain tension in much of Browne's work. It lies in his reverence for aristocratic good breeding and ancestry, found only 'at home', and the simultaneous conviction of the superiority of Australian colonial life, particularly in the way it leads to physical excellence. In *My Run Home*, as it was called when published as a book in 1897, a colonial pugilist defeats a bigger opponent in a village fight, the author-hero wins a steeplechase, and an Australian girl vanquishes her English rivals even in archery. And yet Browne can write of 'that other England that is growing up in the South' (p. 216), and assert the essential belief that England is more truly home than Australia. His fictional self is able to combine the best of these two worlds by marrying an English cousin and bringing not only his bride but also her family to his Australian property.

'The Wild Australian' (1877) was Browne's only attempt at writing an epistolary novel, and his only serial which was not republished; his small command of characterization allows for the minimum of variety in the letters. In this absurd story a young English squire, Robert Hazelwood, changes places with his Australian friend Philip Cherbury to trick a lady novelist who is looking for an Australian for her next book; Robert behaves outrageously, so that the portrait is grossly misleading; when the secret comes out he is challenged to a duel and wounded by an irascible Australian millionaire. All ends happily, however, with Philip marrying Robert's sister Ella and staying in England; Robert also marries, and so does the lady novelist. The story indicates Browne's conflicting Anglo-Australian attitude more interestingly than *My Run Home*, as he shows by the action that an Englishman's presentation of a gauche Australian is unconvincing to a real Australian, and therefore mistaken in its conception, whereas the Australian is able to pass himself off as an upper-class Englishman with success. This is one of his few stories in which the hero does not touch Australia; it begins in India then moves to England, and the only really Australian ingredient is John Bedwin, a squatter of Quondong, who writes to Philip saying that England may be attractive, but he is supremely happy where he is, on the land and under an open sky.

The next three serials, 'An Australian Squire' (1879), 'The Miner's Right' (1880) and 'Robbery Under Arms' (1882-83), all have Australian settings, but then Browne turned to imaginative romance again in 1884 with 'The Sealskin Mantle', published in the *Sydney Mail* (1884-85) and in hard covers as *The Sealskin Cloak* in 1889. The story turns on the supposed death in a train crash of Marguerite, the beautiful wife of a rich Englishman, Hugh Gordon; however, the body of a passenger to whom she had given her sealskin cloak has been mistaken for hers. After Hugh has remarried, Marguerite reappears under the name of Madame Latour; she becomes a governess, first to her own two children, then with the wealthy Baldhills, who take her back to their Australian property. The voyage includes a trip up the Nile, a battle between Arab tribesmen and much beautiful scenery. The action of the last hundred pages takes place at the Baldhills' Sydney mansion and their country station. Marguerite and Hugh are finally able to marry again and they settle in Australia. Nearly half of *The Sealskin Cloak* is taken up by the Egyptian episodes, and the frail plot, composed of implausibly connected events, supports an improbable tale of travel and adventure. The writing is of uneven quality, adequate when describing scenery, empty and inflated when trying to cope with emotion; the story swings from highly wrought melodrama to jolly descriptions of station life, 'with late dinners, tennis, four-in-hand driving, shooting, and kangaroo coursing, billiards and occasionally whist thrown in' (p. 441). The English who stay outback are as delighted with the charm of Australian bush life as they are astonished at the sophistication of the city. One gentleman complains that it is even ' "Too much like England, that's the worst of it" ' (p. 414)—the kind of remark which typifies the ambivalent attitude found in so many of Browne's novels.

A continuing concern with the conflict implied here underlies the plot of 'The Final Choice' (1885), later called *The Crooked Stick*, in which Pollie Devereux, the heiress of Corindah station, is about to marry her English cousin, Bertram, when she learns he is to all intents betrothed to Sybil de Wynton, of Wynton Hall, Herefordshire. He returns to England, wealth and his rightful bride and Pollie marries the faithful Australian squatter, Harold Atherstone. The writing is again melodramatic at emotional moments, but the book's greatest weakness is in the sudden change in Bertram from a likeable new chum gaining colonial experience to an utter cad who deceives innocent women.

'Nevermore', a *Centennial Magazine* serial of 1889-90, is a stronger work. It is the best of the romances because Browne used for his background and characters places and types with which he was familiar personally, not merely imaginatively. The hero, Lance Trevanion, again a well-born Englishman, leaves home to seek his fortune on the Victorian goldfields, swearing to return in five years and marry his cousin Estelle Chaloner. On the voyage out he discovers a *doppelgänger* on board, the evil Lawrence Trevenna. They quarrel, and Trevenna vows vengeance. Lance has luck on the Ballarat goldfields, but is too naïve to see that his friendship with the horse-stealing Lawless family, Ned, Dan and especially Kate, is dangerous. They also take up with Trevenna. When Lance is arrested for owning a stolen horse he knocks down Dayrell the trooper and is sentenced to two years hard labour. While in gaol he retaliates against a sadistic warder and is sent to the hulks in Williamstown Bay. Tess Lawless, Ned's cousin, contrives his escape and he goes to the Omeo goldfields where he is again successful but falls in with bad company, taking as his partner an old villain, Caleb Coke, who goes cattle-duffing with Trevenna, now married to Kate. Trevenna and Coke murder Lance, and Trevenna passes himself off to the newly arrived Estelle as her fiancé, though she instinctively suspects him. Kate discovers the murder, rides exhaustingly to a police station and Dayrell is able to arrest Trevenna at the marriage altar. Estelle returns to England, and on the death of Lance's father it is discovered that Trevenna had been his natural son.

There are clear links with *For the Term of his Natural Life* in 'Nevermore', most obviously the use of a double as a mainspring of the plot, and the hero's experiences as a prisoner, but Browne's tale lacks the depth and essentially tragic vision of Clarke's novel in its revised form. The idea of class ostensibly underlies much of the action. In court, for instance, Lance declares that since he is 'a gentleman of good, indeed ancient family' (p. 80) it would be impossible for him to be involved in horse-stealing. In prison he works among 'the prison herd' (p. 127) and his adversary Bracker is a 'child of the masses' (p. 129). Lawrence Trevenna, like Gloucester's Edmund, is a bastard son and therefore wicked. Education, too, is important—the Lawless family are illiterate, and their good cousin, Tess, does their writing for them. Despite himself, however, Browne presents arguments against his theory of aristocracy. Lance's good breeding is of no use in his new conditions on the goldfields; he is blinded by innocence to the dangers he meets, even though he is warned by the lowly-born gold-miners he works with. Dayrell is at first an unusual character for Browne to create, since he is an unsympathetically presented policeman; hungry for a conviction, he gets one by deceiving a woman, Kate Lawless, and manipulating her emotions. Later in the book, however, he becomes the stock figure of the trusty trooper. Kate, Tess and the other women on the goldfields are comparatively credible, and even Estelle is often less stilted than her counterparts in other Browne stories.

While there are plenty of the usual melodramatic sentimental passages, there are also several which excite by their liveliness. Browne is often at his best when writing out of his own experience. Here, for instance, the two trial scenes and Kate Lawless's final ride through the bush have a clarity and vigour which so much of his writing lacks owing to his artificial, high-flown vocabulary. *Nevermore* is more satisfactory than, say, *The Sealskin Cloak* at least partly because the setting is mainly working-class and the dialogue cannot afford to be too unrealistic without becoming incongruous. Browne was concerned with realism, but in setting, action and lower-class characters rather than in emotions, which are usually expressed in improbable rhetoric.

The Lawless family, modelled on the Kellys, attracted Browne, for he used them again during the opening chapters of another romance with a mining background, *The Ghost Camp* (1902), when an old Scot tells the hero, Valentine Blount, what amounts to the story of *Nevermore* continued to its conclusion in which Dayrell and Ned are both killed in a gun battle, and Kate and her youngest brother, Dick, disappear into Queensland. The main story of the novel concerns Blount's successful mining career in Tasmania and his marriage to a grazier's sister-in-law, Imogen Carrisforth. They enjoy society life in Hobart, and just before they leave for England, Blount learns that he has inherited the title and estates of the Earl of Fontenaye. The book contains much self-indulgent imagining by the author, but occasionally he strikes a deeper, more conflicting note. At the end of Chapter VII a Tasmanian squatter is asked if he looks forward to retiring to England, to live comfortably on the rents from his properties. He replies that the colonist, after a few years, has 'an inevitable feeling of loneliness in Europe, which he cannot shake off' (p. 234); the Englishman going home has his family and friends to go to, and even then he often returns to Australia, where there is something attractive in the freer life. Browne presents Tasmania as a miniature England, and its social life only slightly less glittering than what might be expected in London and the counties. His squatters and their ladies are, generally, satisfied with the situation. But the truly nobly born, those from an ancient line, usually return to claim their inheritance, as Valentine Blount does, or die, like Lance Trevanion.

The Lawless family appears again in Browne's final work, *The Last Chance* (1905), a romance of greater fantasy than any of the earlier novels—a transparently imagined piece of wish-fulfilment. Arnold Banneret, the hero, is a Goldfields Commissioner at Burrawang, New South Wales, who leaves his job, goes mining in Western Australia and becomes one of the wealthiest men in Australia. One evening an armed robbery is foiled by a young miner who is, however, wounded and dies revealing that he is really Dick Lawless. The Last Chance mine continues to pour forth its golden stream: the Bannerets go 'home', buy the estate of the impoverished Lord Hexham and astonish British society by their polish and generosity. (Browne had considered 'Saxemundham' as the title, but rejected it for the more simple 'Hexham'). One son, Reggie, marries Corisande, the daughter of Lord Hexham, and intends to return to Western Australia to supervise the mining company.

The book meanders from one cloudless event to the next, and includes more literary references than any other of Browne's novels. As well as the inevitable Scott, among the authors mentioned or quoted are Jane Austen, Kipling, Wordsworth, the Brontës and Marcus Clarke. There is an arch reference to *Robbery Under Arms*, but the most curious use of another book is an inserted story about Captain William Hayston, a South Sea Island adventurer who is the central figure of *A Modern Buccaneer*, published ten years previously. The digression has almost no connection with the main plot, which is in any case little more than a sequence of events. Although this last novel has small literary merit, it has a certain autobiographical interest.

Browne was seventy-eight when he wrote it, and the idealized Goldfields Commissioner is the last of several such characters in his books, most notably William Blake in *The Miner's Right*. Banneret is described as a one-time squatter who had entered the civil service on losing his money when the price of stock had fallen. His success on the goldfields and purchase of an English estate are the splendid dreams which the author attaches to the earlier reality. Browne is still basically unresolved in his attitude to England as an Australian, even though superficially he appears to be firm. He will have no nationalistic nonsense, and has one character speak of 'an Englishman, that is, an Australian, which is all the same, of course' (p. 448). He lauds 'Britain the Unconquered' (p. 172) and yet 130 pages further on has one of his characters objecting to 'unqualified praise of England for being England' (p. 307). The aristocratic structure of society is maintained by the colonial Reggie marrying the daughter of the Earl of Hexham and so restoring to her the family estates; but then they go to live in Western Australia. Perhaps this is the most agreeable compromise that can be expected.

Two of Browne's romances set themselves apart from the others. These are *A Modern Buccaneer* (1894), a South Sea Island adventure with a curious history, and *War to the Knife* (1899), which is set in New Zealand at the time of the Maori Wars. The first is the self-told story of Hilary Telfer who leaves his Sydney home for the sea at seventeen and becomes supercargo with the notorious Captain Bully Hayston, a gentlemanly scoundrel who trades in the South Seas. Incidents occur at the various islands visited, with little plot connection. After a massacre, and a well-described wreck, Telfer leaves Hayston and lives an idyllic and unconvincingly celibate life on one of the islands. Hayston is tracked down by a British man-of-war, and on the evidence of a missionary is charged with illegal activities but escapes; Telfer is exonerated of being an accomplice and returns to Sydney. On the way he is rescued from drowning at Norfolk Island by the beautiful island girl, Miranda, whom he marries and takes to Sydney where they live rich and happy in a charming house beside the harbour. Unlike most of Browne's later work, much of *A Modern Buccaneer* is written in a plain and unembellished style. When the travellers in *The Sealskin Cloak*, for instance, are on the Nile, their visit to the island of Philae is partly described in this way:

> . . . The tide of life has ebbed and flowed since first they saw those high-piled masses of darksome rocks, of weird shape, and strange contour, the silvery sands, the deep-hued verdure, the purple flowers, the

nodding palm plumes, yet till life's current fails and the frosts of age have chilled the pulses of the heart, ne'er can that memory fail. Almost painful was the feeling of surprised rapture which possessed every gazer as through craggy rock and waving foliage the silvern surface of the lake appeared. Lo! in the centre of the charmed water arises the sacred island—an emerald carven to the river's edge—amid the solemn shadows of the temple city. (p. 243)

With this may be compared the following account of a visit by Hayston and Telfer to the Pacific Island of Ponapé:

> . . . the Captain and I spent two days on shore exploring the mysterious ruins and ancient fortifications which render the island so deeply interesting; wonderful in size, Cyclopean in structure. It is a long-buried secret by whom and for what purpose they were erected. None remain to tell. 'Their memorial is perished with them.'
>
> In one of the smaller islands on which those ruins are situated, Hayston told me that a Captain Williams, in 1836, had found over £10,000 worth of treasure. He himself believed that there were rich deposits in other localities not far distant.
>
> To this end we explored a series of deathly cold dungeons, but found nothing except a heavy disc of a metal resembling copper several feet under ground.
>
> This was lying with its face to the stone wall of the subterranean chamber—had lain there probably for centuries.
>
> Its weight was nearly that of fifty pounds. It had three holes in the centre. We could form no idea as to its probable use or meaning. I was unwilling to part with it, however, and taking it on board, put it in my cabin. (pp. 80-1)

Both passages present reactions of wonder and pleasure, but the brisk sentence structure and paragraphing, the factual, unemotional statement and the clear-cut tone of the one are in direct contrast with the romantic, quasi-poetic and artificial rhetoric of the other, which is a fair example of what could be called Browne's heightened style.

The unflattering portraits of the missionary, Morland, and his assistant in *A Modern Buccaneer* are also unusual for Browne. The writing most typical of his work is contained in the first few pages of the book and the last four chapters, which introduce the Shakespearean romance with Miranda, and three characters from Browne's earlier book, *A Colonial Reformer*. All this is not surprising when it is learned that except for one episode, which he borrowed from his father's journals, the rest, about two-thirds of the book in fact, was apparently rewritten by Browne from a manuscript by Louis Becke, at that time trying to establish himself as an author. Becke, who had himself fictionalized the adventures with Hayston retold in the book from his own experiences with the American trader Bully Hayes, sold his manuscript to Browne for £25—half on delivery and half on publication. As Browne received £250 as advance royalties for it, he promised in effect no more than ten per cent of his advance to Becke. In October 1893 Becke wrote to an English correspondent that Browne had offered to write a preface for 'my book', and Becke himself felt that this would ensure a large Australian sale. In September Browne had written to Macmillan saying his next book, *A Modern Buccaneer*, would be ready about December. 'I have read "The Wrecker" ', he wrote, 'and in spite of Mr Stevenson's high reputation, do not anticipate being extinguished by it'.[20] The manuscript was sent off in December, and the book was published in time for copies to reach Albury by 21 May 1894; Browne had some of them sent to Becke, who was astonished to find how much of the book was his own work. He sent off an angry letter to Browne; Banjo Paterson got legal advice for him on how to secure an appropriate acknowledgement; and Browne made this in an advertisement in the *Daily Telegraph* for 13 August 1894. The same acknowledgement appeared in subsequent editions of the book itself.

This is a curious affair. Browne's egotistical and apparently dishonest letters to Macmillan show him in a distinctly unfavourable light. As well, he wrote a letter to the *Book Buyer* in New York, saying that he had acquired 'all right, title and interest' in some notes made by Becke in the Pacific Islands; these, he said, had been used with Becke's knowledge and consent in the preparation of the book; there had been a slight misunderstanding when no acknowledgement had been made, but this had since been rectified.[21] As he had copies of the book sent to Becke when it was published, it seems unlikely that he himself felt that he was being dishonest. The story of Telfer-Becke and Hayston-Hayes is similar in a way to the fictionalized autobiography that had been Browne's method ever since he began writing, and it is just possible that in copying out Becke's manuscript he came to believe that he was really composing it. He saw himself, moreover, as comparable with Kipling and Stevenson, two Macmillan authors whose works appeared in illustrated editions. Despite his repeated requests, none of his own books had ever been given this added attraction, and he now saw himself challenging Stevenson on his own ground; he had to be content, however, with a folding map as a frontispiece. Another pressure still upon him was his continuing debt to his brothers-in-law (his journal entry for 16 May 1898 notes a release of mortgage from Hugh Massie) and to use Becke's manu-script was a quick way to write a story even for so methodical a writer as Browne. It is possible that he was taking advantage of a man he would have considered of a lower class but it is diffi-cult to believe that the fundamentally good-natured and hard-working Browne would be so dishonest. It would be charitable to believe rather that he was naïve. Whatever the truth of the matter the title of the novel is pleasantly ironic.

The idea for the second adventure, *War to the Knife*, may have arisen through his friendship with George Rusden, whose history of New Zealand had been published in a new edition in 1895; it had first appeared in 1883, followed in 1888 by *Aerere-tanga: Groans of the Maoris*. Browne worked from both these books and did some research in the Melbourne Public Library to gather background for his novel which he wrote during 1898, sending it off in August. The highly coloured story begins typically in Massinger Court, Herefordshire. The young heir, Sir Roland de Massinger, has been unsuccessful in his wooing of Hypatia Tollemache and goes off to New Zealand, selling his whole estate to an Australian squatter. He becomes involved in the Maori War of 1860, joining a volunteer army, Von Temp-sky's Forest Rangers, and Hypatia comes to New Zealand to do missionary work. Roland falls in love with a beautiful half-caste, Erena Mannering, but when she dies saving him from certain death he returns to England with Hypatia as his bride and buys back his estates, having conveniently inherited a large fortune. The battles and the bloodthirsty savagery of some of the Maori attacks are described vigorously, but the romantic love story is tedious and full of clichés like 'She gazed on him with the pitying tenderness of womanhood shining through her troubled eyes' (p. 369). There is perhaps some dramatic conflict in the meeting between Erena and Hypatia, but it is dissipated by the inflated style which infects not only much of this book, but much of the writing in all these romances.

The pastoral novels draw largely on Browne's own experience, which he usually places in a romantic framework. After 'The Fencing of Wanderowna' (1873) and 'The Squatter's Dream' (1875), his next serial, 'A Colonial Reformer' (1876-77), was an-other success story of the squattocracy. Ernest Neuchamp of Buckinghamshire migrates with the intention of improving the barbarous colonials. Conquering various difficulties he finally becomes 'one of the largest proprietors in Australia, both of pastoral and urban property' (p. 470), helped by a banker, Paul

Frankston, and a careful squatter, Abstinens Levison, who was modelled on James Tyson, reputedly the richest man in Australia.[22] Levison sells him store cattle and even buys back for him land on his river front which had been free selected by the Freeman brothers. At this period Browne had no time for the selection system, and the Freemans are among the villains of the book. Others, with similarly indicative names, are Hartley Selmore, who tries to swindle Neuchamp into buying the useless Gammon Downs property, Count Albert von Schätterheims, a German adventurer who crowns his villainy by trying to abduct an heiress, and Hardy Baldacre, a slovenly grazier. These allegorical names are appropriate to the generally moral attitude and didactic purpose of the book. The innocent Neuchamp learns by his mistakes under the kindly guidance of Frankston and Levison and is rewarded with prosperity and happiness. Browne includes, incidentally, a great deal of information useful to the man on the land—in much the same way that the author of the radio serial 'Blue Hills' wrote into certain episodes discussion and information on current rural affairs.

'An Australian Squire' (1877-79), republished in 1900 as *Babes in the Bush*, has a greater element of romance and adventure. Browne's earlier serial of 1877, 'The Wild Australian', set in an English county mansion, was a transitional work in that it was completely fictional, and only tenuously related to Australia. 'An Australian Squire' shows how a decayed English gentleman, Howard Effingham—a highly unoriginal, if noble, name—takes his family to Warbrok, a run-down property near Yass, and becomes a successful squatter. Interwoven is the story of Gyp Warleigh, the son of the former dissolute owners of the place, who leads an expedition overlanding cattle across the Alps and is killed in an affray with Aboriginals. He was so admired as a leader that the men called the promised land he led them to 'Gyp's Land' (with no apologies to Governor Gipps).

The importance of education is stressed in this book, through the character of Gyp. He is an excellent bushman, and his regular features plainly show 'the marks of aristocratic lineage' (p. 140), but he has missed out on the education of a gentleman; however, as one of the men (who *is* a gentleman) says, ' "Blood is a great, a tremendous thing; though he doesn't know enough for a sergeant of dragoons, yet there is a grand unconsciousness in his bearing and a natural air of authority . . . which he derives from his family descent" ' (p. 333). And when he dies two volumes are discovered in his pocket, not a novel, but a history of England—he was trying to improve himself. The young

26

squatters in the expedition led by Gyp are all well educated and well read. In 1904 Browne wrote that they 'were chiefly portraits of personal friends' of the Port Fairy days, men of 'birth, breeding and refinement',[23] and the accounts of race meetings, picnics and hunting in 'An Australian Squire' are similar to those in *Old Melbourne Memories*. They are rose and gold reminiscences of happier times twenty years before, and in his closing pages the author describes the station and the Yass district as Arcadia (p. 418), his habitual name for the demi-Paradise.

His next pastoral serial, 'A Sydney-Side Saxon', appeared in 1888-89 after 'The Miner's Right', 'Robbery Under Arms' and 'The Sealskin Mantle'; it shows some of the raciness and economy of the best of these, as well as a little of the melodramatic nonsense of the worst. It is a thinly disguised book of advice to new chums like the hero, Jesse Claythorpe, a farm labourer who emigrates from Kent with his sister Jane; she meets an English squire's alcoholic son, reforms him, and then marries him. Both he and Jesse become successful squatters. The climax of the book is a steeplechase contest between a dashing half-caste, Possum Barker, who has been well brought up by her white father, and Nellie Thoresby, a local squatter's daughter. Jesse has been rather dazzled by Possum, but she is thrown from her horse and dies. Jesse marries Nellie and they have a large family. His children and grandchildren form the audience to whom he is telling the story—though they are referred to only at the beginning and the end of the book, which is a comparatively plain account of incidents in station life, mostly free of the verbose style of the romances. As in *Robbery Under Arms* the style is dictated by the narrator, and there are few frills, but the incidents are unexciting and the story remains dull. The introduction of the half-caste Possum, however, looks forward to the later Erena Mannering of *War to the Knife*; in both instances the hero is attracted by the beauty, intelligence and behaviour of the girl, and in the later book there is a mutual declaration of love, but in each case the young woman dies and the hero marries an eminently suitable white girl. There can be no miscegenation in Arcadia. It is allowable in *A Modern Buccaneer*, because Miranda is several generations away from her Polynesian ancestor, and 'her complexion was so fair that . . . I might have taken her for an Englishwoman' (p. 234).

The last pastoral romance, *Plain Living* (1898), was the first of Browne's novels to be written after his retirement, and it is flimsier than anything of similar length he had so far produced. It begins autobiographically with the bank foreclosing on the squatter, Harold Stamford, in a drought. Unlike Tom Browne, the hero is able to transfer his mortgage, he inherits £173,000, and it rains. He keeps the legacy secret from his family so that they will not be corrupted by wealth (this is a moral story) but they nevertheless revel in society balls, dinners and the delights of Sydney, where they always stay at Batty's (Browne's sobriquet for Petty's) hotel. A parallel plot shows how the children in another family are corrupted by riches so that the son marries a barmaid and the daughter marries a clerk (and what's more marries him in a registry office); the Stamford children, of course, marry well. This slight, artificial story lacks the informational value of the earlier pastoral novels; as a group these have some interest for the Australian social historian, but there is little, if anything, to recommend *Plain Living* even to the most tolerant reader.

'The Miner's Right' (1880) could have been by a different author. Written during Browne's last years at Gulgong, and immediately before his finest novel, the book frequently captures the vivid excitement and movement of a gold-rush town. The hero is Hereward (Harry) Pole, the younger son of a decayed family, 'gently nurtured, well intentioned, utterly useless' (p. 1); he emigrates to Victoria after plighting his troth with Ruth Allerton, the local squire's daughter, and after four years he and his partners are successful; their claim is jumped and while awaiting a court decision they go to the Oxley goldfields in New South Wales. There, events swiftly follow one upon another. Pole's Australian partner, Cyrus Yorke, is accidentally killed, and there are two murders—the villainous Malgrade, who was behind the claim-jumping, is stabbed by his wife Dolores, and Jane Mangold, who had followed Pole from England, is slain by her husband Morsley. Pole is charged with the crime but acquitted. He is also involved in a gold escort robbery and the Chinese riots at Green Gully, and finally leaves the diggings for Sydney, where he discovers that the Allertons have sailed out from England; he marries Ruth and they make a trip to the goldfields before returning to Kent, leaving all Harry's friends happy and prosperous—even the Goldfields Commissioner, Blake, inherits a fortune.

Writing for the most part from his immediate experience, and using as character material the people he saw every day, Browne here approaches his truest vein. The aristocratic framework is still there and Harry Pole is always the gentleman of the story, but he merges himself with his working-class companions much more than Lance Trevanion was to do in *Nevermore* some years later. He almost becomes a believable character. He does not, finally, because Browne could see into the mind of an English gentleman on the goldfields only with his romantic imagination. So it is that characters like Cyrus Yorke and his wife, even at times Jane Mangold, are more convincing. The Goldfields Commissioner, William Blake, is firmly drawn even though it is an idealized self-portrait.

The depiction of the mining community is on the whole kindly, and although it was claimed in 1910 by a local journalist that real people were thinly disguised under fictitious names and that the book was 'monstrously misleading',[24] it is more likely that Browne drew his characters from several models rather than individuals. Modifying the methods used in his reminiscences for the magazines, he often invites identification of characters and places by making very slight alteration or none at all; and some of these were certainly local—the good-hearted shopkeepers in the book are the Mangroves, for instance, while the postmistress at Gulgong was Mrs Angove. The 'Oxley goldfields' have a fictitious name, and the riots against the Chinese at Lambing Flat in 1861 are diluted in their change to Green Gully, but the Frank Gardiner holdup of the Forbes gold escort in June 1862 did occur at Eugowra Rocks. Campbell and Keightley (p. 246) were real settlers who shot bushrangers, but the names of the bushrangers themselves are slightly changed. Dunn, Gardiner and Hall become Gunn, Lardner and Wall, for example, and their hideout is in the Yeddin instead of the Weddin mountains. Incidents, however, are at times less fictionalized than the romantic traditions which have grown up around them. The shooting down of Ben Hall as described in Chapter XXVIII, for example, is closer to the police report than to local legend, which holds that he was shot while asleep. According to official records, Hall was called upon to give himself up, but started to run for cover instead. He was then shot in the back with a shotgun, and again by a repeating rifle. Browne adds the detail that Hall shot his revolver twice, and so puts the police in a better light. His account of Gardiner's escape, trial, imprisonment and eventual freedom is factual: Gardiner became a storekeeper in Queensland on his escape, was captured, tried, gaoled and finally allowed to settle in America.

These were incidents that Browne read in the newspapers and discussed with other magistrates and police officers, but many of the goldfields incidents came from his own first-hand knowledge. Almost as soon as he arrived in Gulgong a claim-jumping case came before the bench and, as in the book, the defendants gained an injunction against the complainants' working the claim. A month later a letter in the *Gulgong Guardian* stated that Browne had given diametrically opposed verdicts in exactly similar cases.[25] He was learning to handle a difficult but not uncommon situation, and his description of it in the book shows how well he learned. The killing of Jane Mangold may be traced to William Bell's stabbing of his wife and her lover in September 1871; even though the victims survived in that case, the circumstances as described in the *Guardian* are not dissimilar, and there was a great deal of blood, as in the murder of Jane. The button from the murderer's coat which is found in Jane's hand is exactly like the evidence which convicted a shepherd of murdering a girl at Coonabarabran in the 1870s and recalled by Browne in the *Life* series 'Wild Deeds of Wild Days in Australia' in 1905. An even closer parallel is found in the death of a miner reported in the *Guardian* for 4 November 1871 and Cyrus Yorke's death in Chapter XXIV. The miner, James Geddes, mistakenly thought the rope was attached to the whimhorse, which hauled the rope up and down, and descended unchecked 140 feet to the bottom of the shaft. He was brought to the surface and died three days later. Cyrus mistakenly thinks he has spragged the rope (that is, inserted a stick to control the speed), and he too dies, the next morning. Browne tightens the action by shortening the time between the accident and death, and makes the incident more plausible by drawing Cyrus as a careless, dim-witted fellow. Earlier in the book Browne describes the descent down a mineshaft and the awful death if any of various accidents should occur. 'In this instance', he continues, 'Cyrus was not fated to illustrate any of these dismal theories' (p. 23). There is some slight preparation here for the accident when it comes, and the understated pathos of the whole event makes it much more successful than the usual death scenes that Browne contrives.

The court sequences are also dramatically effective, even though the changes from direct to indirect speech which Browne makes without apparent reason can be irritating. The fiery little lawyer for the defendants, Dr Bellair, becomes a credible character, through his language and manner, and his exchanges with Blake, the magistrate, have an authority lacking in much of Browne's writing.[26] The appearance in court of Mrs Yorke, Cyrus's wife, has a warmth and humour that springs from her personality as much as from the situation, and as a result she is far more convincing than the delicate and refined Ruth Allerton.

30

The detailed yet economical picture of the goldfields make it difficult to accept the lush, 'poetical' descriptions of places once Pole leaves the Oxley. Sometimes, however, gardens and forests have an almost symbolic value in Browne, as places where visions can happen, where a character can most nearly realize his true self, where important events take place. In *Robbery Under Arms*, for instance, Dick particularly notices how the garden round the old hut has been cared for while he has been in gaol, and the forest provides a distinctive atmosphere to passages in *Babes in the Bush*, *Nevermore* and *War to the Knife*. Towards the end of *The Miner's Right*, Pole comes upon a decaying harbour-side mansion surrounded by a luxuriant overgrown garden. He has a momentary overwhelming memory of Allerton Court and he sinks down 'in freshly-summoned agony of spirit' (p. 320). A few days later Ruth and her parents arrive from England and visit the garden, which they have seen from the ship. Pole has returned, but is not recognized in the dusk; he hears Ruth speak of how she has dreamed of meeting him in such a place. They leave, he seeks them out next day and returns there with her—'I had realised the ancestral paradise', he says (p. 336). It is a common enough image, and the descriptive writing approaches banality, yet there is a peculiar power in this ending to the story. For a moment the reader is reminded of Patrick White's Voss and Laura Trevelyan, in a similar garden. Browne cannot leave it there, though; the goldfields must be visited again and Pole and Ruth have to go home to take up their English estate. At one stage in the writing it might have been otherwise, for Pole identifies himself as an Australian (p. 336), but the author's Anglophilia was here stronger than his patriotism and the hero returns successful to his homeland.

The Miner's Right was second only to *Robbery Under Arms* as a popular and commercial success. Keast Burke lists seventeen editions or reprints in his invaluable bibliography. It was serialized in 1880 both in Australia, in the *Town and Country Journal*, and in England in Silver & Co.'s weekly, *The Colonies and India*. A three-volume edition appeared in April 1890 and the first single-volume edition the following October. One percipient reviewer regretted the lost opportunity for pruning, saying it would have been received 'with far greater warmth and effusion if it had been weeded of something like two-thirds of its original bulk'.[27] Certainly one or other of the Malgrade-Dolores/Morsley-Jane plots is unnecessary. But only in *Robbery Under Arms* did Browne alter the shape of a book in its transition from serial to hard covers, and then it was at the publisher's suggestion. In 1901 Browne was delighted to learn that parts of his mining story had been included in a school reader— Macmillan's Australasian Readers Book VI included Chapters XVI and XVII, and Book V included not only parts of Chapters V and XIII, but part of *A Colonial Reformer* as well.[28] In preparing these extracts for school use, the publishers smoothed out the vernacular of the originals, but Browne made no comment about that. More recently in 1969 *The Miner's Right* was adapted for radio and serialized by the Australian Broadcasting Commission.

In its style, incident and characterization, *The Miner's Right* was a preparation for *Robbery Under Arms*. Harry Pole as narrator frequently tells his story in the common language of everyday educated speech; like most of Browne's heroes he is a well-born Englishman. In *Robbery Under Arms*, however, Captain Starlight cannot tell the story because he has to die a romantic villain-hero's death; by happy accident, or possibly by choice, Browne made his narrator non-heroic and native-born, a man telling his story in the colloquial style of the Australian labourer of the period. Apart from the hero, the characters are drawn not from the author's romantic imagination but from his own environment.

It is not surprising that the first two chapters were rejected by the *Australasian* and the *Town and Country Journal*, for they were quite different from anything Browne had produced before. The beginning is melancholy, since the story is presented as the reminiscences of Dick Marston, the only survivor of an outlaw gang, written while he is in prison waiting to be hanged. The adventure starts when Dick and his brother Jim are led by their father, old Ben, first into cattle-duffing and eventually into bushranging with the mysterious Captain Starlight. They leave their mother and sister Aileen on their small selection at Rocky Flat to join Starlight in droving a mob of stolen cattle from New South Wales to Adelaide, where it is sold. Staying in Melbourne on the way home, Jim falls in love with Jeanie Morrison and Dick becomes entangled with her sister, Kate, even though he knows he loves Gracey Storefield, the daughter of the next farm to their own. After they return to New South Wales Dick and Starlight are taken, tried and put into Berrima gaol; on their escape they turn from cattle-duffing to the more criminal bushranging, holding up coaches, robbing banks and raiding homesteads. Their exploits are planned and carried out from Terrible Hollow, a splendid valley with a secret entrance. They go straight for a time, becoming successful miners on the Turon, and Jeanie comes up to marry Jim. Kate has married unhappily and she and her husband, old Mullockson, keep an hotel on the goldfields. She tries to seduce Dick, but betrays them all on discovering that he still loves Gracey. Starlight, Jim and Dick are making their way up to Queensland and eventual escape to America when they meet Kate again; her vindictiveness, together with the treachery of Starlight's half-caste follower, Warrigal, leads to the deaths of Starlight and Jim and the capture of Dick. His death sentence is transmuted to fifteen years imprisonment, which good behaviour reduces to twelve, and when he finally leaves gaol he marries Gracey; the book ends with them about to go to a Queensland cattle station.

Browne claimed in 1894 that the Marstons were drawn from life; 'The father was an assigned servant, and they were all capital workers', he said, adding that the young man in his story 'Five Men's Lives for one Horse' was also a Marston.[29] Certainly they are more vividly realized than any other of Browne's main characters and the boys are the first notable portraits of native-born colonials in Australian writing. Browne had frequently extolled the physical excellence, intelligence, bravery, manliness and working capacity of the Australian, but the nearest he had come to making him a major figure was in Cyrus Yorke, who is unintelligent and killed off halfway through the story, almost as if he could not be allowed to challenge the aristocratic English hero. The most admirable characters of Browne's short stories and recollections are invariably well-read gentlemen and Jim Marston considers that he and Dick would not have taken to 'cross work' if they had been better educated. The brothers are different enough to be individual; Dick the more impetuous but more fatalistic; Jim the quiet bushman, loving and chivalrous, but too biddable. Their father, old Ben, is like a weathered tree, obstinate and authoritative, at times even more powerful than Starlight himself, as when he brings Moran, Burke, and the others into the gang. And then Starlight himself, elegant, witty, carrying the secret of his past beyond his hero's death. Where in Browne's other novels the fascination of the aristocracy often leads to ludicrous unreality, here it provides a tension between the hero and the other characters. More importantly, it allows for a believable range of behaviour in Starlight himself. He can be the new chum squatter down from the country to sell his cattle in Adelaide, the gallant 'with his soft voice and pleasant smile, which no woman . . . could fight against long' (p. 229), the gentleman digger of the Turon goldfields, the leader who can look at his men 'as if he was their king, with his eyes burning up at last with that slow fire that lay at the bottom of 'em' (p. 410). Whether robbing a lady of a gold watch, entertaining Maddie and Bella Barnes in their father's inn, or dying in the Queensland bush, he is always a gentleman and 'far and away the best man we've ever known' (p. 486), as Dick says. This paradox of the good man who is nevertheless a wrongdoer is a basic strength in the book because it invites the reader to take a moral attitude against his better judgement: we know that Starlight is bad according to the law, but we admire him for his courage, skill and authority. The only thoroughly evil character is the snaky-eyed Moran, modelled on the cruellest of the bushrangers of the sixties, 'Mad Dan' Morgan, who was probably insane. Dick moralizes occasionally, 'Couldn't we all have done well, if the devils of idleness and easy-earned money and false pride had let us alone?' (p. 315), but the responsibility for the boys' turning to crime is taken from them to an extent, being laid first on their father, and then on fate, for it is the toss of a coin which decides them to join Starlight and Ben.

Starlight is an original characterization in a traditional mould which includes Macheath, Turpin and Duval, but his exploits were modelled on those of several real men, especially, according to Browne, 'an undeveloped bushranger—part horse-thief— known as "Midnight", in the Gulgong and Dubbo district'.[30] Midnight's real name was unknown, and police told Browne that he would not reveal it even as he lay dying. Nearly all the other characters are more completely fleshed than those in the rest of Browne's writing. The squatter's daughter, Miss Falkland, is stilted, but Aileen Marston is surprisingly strongly drawn for a representative of holy goodness—this is not a mawkish sketch, for she becomes a recognizable figure through the relationships which develop between herself, the rest of her family and Starlight. The real success in the minor characters are the Barnes girls, Bella and especially Maddie. Warm and lively, they almost bounce off the page.

The major incidents in the story are based on fact. Some, like Rainbow's winning the Turon Handicap, were from Browne's own experience; others were recounted to him by people involved: the siege of the Campbell homestead at Goimbla which was in the original serial (the publishers sensibly advised him to omit it from the book)[31] was recounted to him by Mr Campbell, when the Brownes were staying with him in 1869; for most of the incidents, however, he drew on newspaper reports and probably conversations with friends and relatives. Like

Shakespeare in his histories, Browne transposes people and events with no close regard for the truth. Ben Hall, for instance, worked from a base in the Weddin Mountains in the Central West and had no dealings with Morgan in the Riverina, but Browne's Moran becomes the leader of a gang which includes Wall and Hulbert (Gilbert). His geography is similarly confusing, as he uses the names of real places in impossible relationships. The Turon diggings are in the Bathurst district, and the Barnes' inn is clearly intended to be in the Southern Highlands, 'near the Shoalhaven country' (p. 232), yet it is only a few hours ride away (p. 379). In reality these areas are about 200 miles apart, and much of the country between is wild and rugged. Local tradition has it that the model for the Barnes' inn was the Hen and Chickens inn just outside Bathurst on the Perthville road. Owing to its position and formation, Burragorang Valley has been claimed as the original of Terrible Hollow, the bush-rangers' hideout, but Browne himself stated that the model was a valley in the Gwydir district of New England, which he had read about in a newspaper report.[32] This amalgam of the real and the imaginary results in a highly convincing landscape, which contributes to the book's remarkable unity.

Groups of images have a similar function, and the bush and its creatures provide material for those most commonly used. On the first page Dick says he can 'swim like a musk-duck' and is 'as active as a rock-wallaby'; sometimes a comparison has an apt originality—'Moran's face grew as black as an ironbark tree after a bush fire' (p. 556), for instance, and a forest can look 'as black by night as if all the tree-trunks were cast-iron and the leaves gun-metal' (p. 232). A contrasting set of images is drawn from the drama. Events are not infrequently 'as good as a play' (p. 317), Moran 'looks like the villain on the stage' (p. 490) and Starlight compares his life to a melodrama—' "Enter first robber," and so on' (p. 405). By reference to this artificial presentation of life the characters draw attention to their own realism, and the result, though probably not deliberate on Browne's part, is similar to Brecht's *V-effekt* in the theatre. Another motif is the mopoke, which gives its mournful cry at several moments of crisis, sounding a note of warning, or of doom.[33] But it is the horse which recurs most importantly. Browne was always keen and knowledgeable about horses, and his understanding love for them finds its clearest expression here. The drumming of hoofbeats reverberates throughout the pages of *Robbery Under Arms* and the movement of horses is like a strong current, continually present. It is a horse that sways Jim to join his father and Starlight; it is on horseback that he saves Miss Falkland, whose father later helps Dick; it is a horse that betrays Starlight, when the stolen mare, Locket, is recognized near Cunnamulla; and there is a horse on the last page of the book, the outlaw's splendid Rainbow, 'the best horse in the country', as Maddie says (p. 659).

The action of the book is not unlike the rhythm of a fine horse cantering through the bush, steady and regular, but varied by the events, as a horse's pace is by the terrain. The scenes alternate, with Rocky Flat and Terrible Hollow as fixed poles of good and evil. The sequence of incidents leads the Marston boys into crime gradually, and the intensity of the action increases as they become more deeply involved. First there is merely the disposing of evidence of a stolen calf. Next is the branding of stolen cattle, followed in Chapter XI with the large-scale cattle-duffing venture, based on a similar theft in Queensland by Harry Redford in 1870. After the trial, imprisonment and escape of Starlight and Dick, comes the first robbery under arms; the first period on the Turon is followed by the bank robbery at Ballabri, clearly modelled on the Kellys' hold up of the Jerilderie bank in 1879. Chapter XXVI is both physically and structurally at the centre of the book. Rich in incident, it introduces Moran and Burke, as well as Sir Ferdinand Morringer, the police superintendent; Starlight and the boys move to the Turon, and Kate Mullockson arrives there as well. The Turon is like the inn at Upton in *Tom Jones*; the characters are drawn together and the plot takes on a new direction. Now follows the robbery of the gold escort, bloodshed, murder and the attacks on the station properties, which contrast the gallantry of Starlight and the Marston boys with Moran's churlishness. Then the escape is planned and almost succeeds; Jim and Starlight are shot and Dick is taken, the story ending with his release from gaol and marriage to Gracey Storefield.

The incidents are all different in kind, and the quiet periods in Terrible Hollow which intervene slacken the excitement, making the reader more impatient for the story to continue. Sometimes contrast reinforces the action, as when the murder of the four troopers by Daly and Moran is followed by the gay ironic humour of events at the Turon races, the race ball and Bella Barnes's wedding. The last pages of the book are tranquil after the liveliness and suspense of the escape bid, and contain little sentimentality, and less moralizing.

36

The customary Browne themes are present in *Robbery Under Arms* but not so obtrusively as in the other books. Blood still tells, for example, and Dick is given to statements like 'somehow a man that's born and bred a gentleman will always be different from other men to the end of the world' (p. 59), but there can be no doubt that Browne is glorying in the perilous adventures of bushranging life and the independent ideas of the colonials. Waiting to be hanged, Dick muses, 'A deal of the old life was dashed good fun, and I'd not say, if I had the chance, that I wouldn't do just the same over again' (p. 635). To support his beliefs in good breeding Browne has to falsify his portrait of the police superintendent, Morringer, whose real-life counterpart, Sir Frederick Pottinger, ineffectually chased Ben Hall's gang around the Weddin Hills near Grenfell, and was inefficient enough to shoot himself while mounting a coach. The police were ridiculed by contemporary newspapers, as they are in Chapter XLIII, and also in ballads of the day; one of several aimed at Pottinger himself included the lines, 'But the 'ranger proud, he laughed aloud,/And bounding rode away,/While Sir Frederick Pott shut his eyes for a shot/And missed—in his usual way'.[34] It may not have been coincidence that the busiest period of bushranging in New South Wales ended very soon after his demotion and subsequent death in 1864. While a title for the police superintendent was not strictly necessary, the mystery of Starlight's undoubted gentle birth is essential to the whole structure of the novel; it not only permits contrast between the sophisticated behaviour of the hero, the more homely manner and expression of the Marstons, and the uncouthness of Moran, but also allows for the different characterizations Starlight can adopt in his various roles—Charles Carisforth Esquire, Bernard Muldoon, Lieutenant Lascelles and the rest, play-acting which is linked with the theatrical images in the book.

The success of the good, hard-working George Storefield, Gracey's brother, is less obviously stated than similar successes in the pastoral novels, and while there is a certain amount of moralizing, this is mitigated by the fatalistic attitude which grows stronger as the book proceeds—once set on their course, the boys cannot stop themselves sliding downwards; it is always too late. Perhaps it is not so much moralizing as regret, which is found in many ballads of prisoners' repentance. Some bushranging ballads also included warnings, after their account of brave and daring deeds.[35] Browne himself answered the charge that 'books like *Robbery Under Arms* have a tendency to injure the moral sense of boys'[36] by quoting one of Aileen's denunciations of the

37

Marstons' dishonest life, implying that the sorrow and remorse expressed by Dick are indications of the feelings of real men under similar circumstances, and therefore not an inducement to take up crime. In the book the fatalism is balanced by the constant hope for a future escape from Australia, Starlight married to Aileen, Dick to Gracey, and Jim with his Jeanie:

> Starlight had plenty of money, besides his share of the gold. If we could ever get away from this confounded rock-walled prison, good as it was in some ways; and if he and Aileen and the rest of us could make a clean dart of it and get to America, we could live there free and happy yet, in spite of all that had come and gone. (p. 479)

One of the major achievements of the book is its consistency of tone. This is largely due to its colloquial language, which Browne controls so much better than the imagined rhetoric of high romance which he frequently attempts elsewhere. Alternatively it could be said that he is controlled by the language, for his strong regard for realism prevented the use of his particular kind of 'literary' vocabulary, except for the press reports in which the bushrangers read with amusement of their own doings:

'BUSHRANGERS!
'STARLIGHT AND THE MARSTONS AGAIN

> 'The announcement will strike our readers, if not with the most profound astonishment, certainly with considerable surprise, that these celebrated desperadoes, for whose apprehension such large sums have been offered, for whom the police in all the colonies have made such unremitting search, should have been discovered in our midst. Yet such is the case. On this very morning, from information received, our respected and efficient Inspector of Police, Sir Ferdinand Morringer, proceeded soon after midnight to the camp of Messrs. Clifford and Hastings. He had every reason to believe that he would have had no difficulty in arresting the famous Starlight, who, under the cognomen of the Honourable Frank Haughton, has been for months a partner in this claim. The shareholders were popularly known as "the Three Honourables," it being rumoured that both Mr. Clifford and Mr. Hastings were entitled to that prefix, if not to a more exalted one.
>
> 'With characteristic celerity, however, the famous outlaw had shortly before quitted the place, having received warning and been provided with a fast horse by his singular retainer, Warrigal, a half-caste native of the colony, who is said to be devotedly attached to him, and who has been seen from time to time on the Turon. (pp. 399-400)

Contrasted with this, Dick Marston's flat, even banal, writing can sometimes be a virtue, allowing actions, for example, to be more important than the words describing them. Part of his account of the Ballabri bank hold-up provides an illustration:

. . . Starlight rode up to the bank first. It was about ten minutes to three o'clock. Jim and I popped our horses into the police stables, and put on a couple of their waterproof capes. The day was a little showery. Most of the people we heard afterwards took us for troopers from some other station on the track of bush-rangers, and not in regular uniform. It wasn't a bad joke, though, and the police got well chaffed about it.

We dodged down very careless like to the bank, and went in a minute or two after Starlight. He was waiting patiently with the cheque in his hand till some old woman got her money. She counted it, shillings, pence, and all, and then went out. The next moment Starlight pushed his cheque over. The clerk looks at it for a moment, and quick-like says, 'How will you have it?'

'This way,' Starlight answered, pointing his revolver at his head, 'and don't you stir or I'll shoot you before you can raise your hand.'

The manager's room was a small den at one side. They don't allow much room in country banks unless they make up their mind to go in for a regular swell building. I jumped round and took charge of the young man. Jim shut and locked the front door while Starlight knocked at the manager's room. He came out in a hurry, expecting to see one of the bank customers. When he saw Starlight's revolver, his face changed quick enough, but he made a rush to his drawer where he kept his revolver, and tried to make a fight of it, only we were too quick for him. Starlight put the muzzle of his pistol to his forehead and swore he'd blow out his brains there and then if he didn't stop quiet. (pp. 306-7)

The book is a rich source of Australian expression of the period, for the language is warm, homely and living, as in this description of the bush telegraph, Billy the Boy:

'It's all right,' says father. 'The old dog knowed him; it's Billy the Boy. There's something up.'

Just as he spoke we saw a horseman come in sight; and he rattled down the stony track as hard as he could lick. He pulled up just opposite the house, close by where we were standing. It was a boy about fifteen, dressed in a ragged pair of moleskin trousers, a good deal too large for him, but kept straight by a leather strap round the waist. An old cabbage-tree hat and a blue serge shirt made up the rest of his rig. Boots he had on, but they didn't seem to be fellows, and one rusty spur. His hair was like a hay-coloured mop, half-hanging over his eyes, which looked sharp enough to see through a gum tree and out at the other side. (p. 245)

It can sustain a genuinely poetic feeling, as in the account of the night ride from Berrima gaol in Chapter XX, picture an event like the Eugowra escort robbery with brief, sharp strokes, and provide a succinct portrait like this one of Starlight:

> Nobody knew who he'd been, or almost where he had come from—next to nothing about him had ever come out. He was an Englishman—that was certain—but he must have come young to the colony. No one could look at him for a moment and see his pale, proud face, his dark eyes—half-scornful, half-gloomy, except when he was set up a bit (and then you didn't like to look at them at all)—without seeing that he was a gentleman to the tips of his delicate-looking fingers, no matter what he'd done, or where he'd been.
>
> He was rather over the middle size; because he was slight made, he always looked rather tall than not. He was tremendous strong, too, though he didn't look that, and as active as a cat, though he moved as if walking was too much trouble altogether, and running not to be thought of. (pp. 478-9)

The story appeared at an opportune time. The Kellys had been rounded up and Ned hanged less than two years before, and the exploits of Gardiner, Hall, Gilbert and Dunn were only twenty years behind. Even though set in the 1850s, the various events of the plot were recognizably those of ten and fifteen years later. It attracted readers of all kinds. W. E. Gladstone thanked the publishers of the first edition for sending him 'a work of so much interest and such conspicuous talent'. Henry Lawson recorded that as a lad he read Dickens, Marryat, Bret Harte 'And oh! of course we read *Robbery Under Arms* when it first appeared in the *Sydney Mail*'—he was fifteen at the time. In 1905 Browne recalled that on a train journey he had once met a squatter who had told him how he used to read each weekly instalment to the station hands as it came. One week there was no paper, and there was such consternation that he had 'wired to the postmaster at the township to let us know how "Starlight" had got on'.[37] Its popularity led to a dramatized version by Alfred Dampier and Garnet Walch in 1890, and Dampier chose it for his farewell Melbourne performance before going to England in 1894, where he also produced it. Other versions were staged, including one as late as 1917, and it has been filmed at least three times, by Australian producers in 1907 and 1920 and by the Rank organization in 1957. In 1966 it was serialized for radio by the Australian Broadcasting Commission.

Whether deliberately or not, Browne correctly seized on the Irish element in the bushranging gangs—names of real outlaws like Dunn, Bourke, O'Meally, Kelly, Byrne are sufficient to indicate their predominance—and Aileen Marston's Catholicism leads her eventually into a convent (although it was not going to prove any obstacle to her marriage with Starlight). Browne is sympathetic towards the Marstons and their class, but clearly shows, by the example of George Storefield, what the Australian farmer can achieve by hard work and careful management. He can even rise to become a Member of Parliament along with the squatter who has been there, in his rightful place, all the time. He can, indeed, become a Gentleman.

The principal reasons for the literary success of *Robbery Under Arms*, then, lie in the use of a lower-class narrator, which restrains Browne's style, the realistic re-creation of events, and the tight, unified construction. The action is varied and suspense is maintained so that the reader wants to know what is going to happen next. Browne has the end of the story with the deaths of four men firmly in view from the start, but occasional inconsistencies occur. Patsey Daly, for instance, is hanged on page 13 and shot on page 546; Billy the Boy is clearly known to Starlight on page 120, but meets him for the first time on page 245; and Starlight and the Marstons have spent their last night together drinking bad grog at the 'Willow Tree shanty' on page 4 while in Chapter XLIX Dick and Jim don't even see their leader at the shanty, now called the Traveller's Rest; on their last desperate night together they are trying to escape through the bush.

Lapses of this kind are worth noting because they are unusual in Browne; they may indicate his close involvement with the action of the moment and his more stimulated creativity in relation to *Robbery Under Arms* generally. It was produced when the author was fifty-six years of age and at the midpoint of his writing career. Behind him were seven other serials, two pastoralists' handbooks and enough shorter pieces for two volumes; still to come were four more serials, five novels, two novelettes and some short stories. He never again tried to write in the same style, and he never again wrote with such assurance, economy and verve. His success may have influenced other writers to use bushranging as a subject during the early twentieth century—Ambrose Pratt, for example, published three semi-historical narratives about bushrangers, one in 1905 and two in 1911—but none of their work has the literary quality of Dick Marston's story.

Before the publication of *Robbery Under Arms* by Macmillan in June 1889 Browne's writing was known only to an Australian audience and to some English readers interested in the colonies. One reviewer of the Remington edition of 1888 considered that 'the story is one of mere vulgar ruffianism; and the plan on which it is written, the whole being told in the slang and rough language of an Australian bushranger, makes it exceedingly tedious to read'.[38] This was not, however, the popular view. Twelve months later the book had begun a career which made Rolf Boldrewood a well-known author in England and North America as well as Australia, and led to the publication of almost everything he had written and was to write.

Informed opinion has in general praised *Robbery Under Arms* and dismissed the rest of Browne's fiction except for *The Miner's Right, The Squatter's Dream* and, more recently, *Nevermore.* Some critics have been misled by their belief that *Robbery Under Arms* was his first novel. Nettie Palmer, for instance, considered in 1924 that the success of the English edition 'led to his writing for an overseas public, and his other books were more occupied in showing off Australia to an outside audience', and this error was repeated as late as 1961 when H. M. Green considered that he 'wrote largely for English readers'.[39] It would be more accurate to say that he wrote for Australian readers whom he judged by his own attitudes, including the belief that Australia could be another England, so far as a landed ruling class was concerned. Earlier commentators mostly remarked favourably on the swing and gusto of *Robbery Under Arms*, the lively action and the description of the country, but Desmond Byrne's comments in his *Australian Writers* (1896) had more insight—he noticed, for instance, that the use of an uneducated narrator led to the repression of the worst faults of Browne's usual style. It was often ranked with Clarke's and Kingsley's work as representing Australia's most distinctive writing, but Browne's cheerful optimism was contrasted with Clarke's morbidity. Green brought a new note to comment on Browne when he remarked in his *Outline of Australian Literature* (1930) that Dick Marston was 'perhaps the first thoroughly Australian character in fiction' (p. 55), but Jim, Billy the Boy and the Barnes girls could well be added, and in an essay published in 1947 Green certainly included Jim in his statement. Two years later Dr Thomas Wood was the first to comment positively on the vocabulary, the ingredient of the book which he liked best, thus turning the complete circle begun by the reviewer of 1888. More recent criticism includes a reassessment, which contains several inaccuracies, by Clive Hamer, who finds Browne's style 'at best unimpressive and at its worst ungrammatical, ostentatious, verbose', and two carefully researched articles by R. B. Walker on the use of historical material in *The Miner's Right* and *Robbery Under Arms*.[40]

Browne has value as a sympathetic recorder of the pastoral

society of the 1850s and 1860s, especially of western Victoria, and books like *The Miner's Right* and *Nevermore* are rich in detail of mining life. His romantic novels are examples of current fashion, not noticeably good, and occasionally, as in *War to the Knife*, downright bad. He is best when he writes of historical events and from his own experience, worst when he writes of what he knows only in his imagination. He was primarily a journalist who aimed to please the public because he needed to make money; in this he succeeded, moderately before Macmillan published *Robbery Under Arms*, and then beyond all his hopes and expectations. In March 1892, for instance, he received cheques for £1,620 from Macmillan, and £250 was the usual advance on his books, a dozen of which were published after that date.

His sternly middle-class attitude was of course counter to the growing force of Australian political and literary thought. One of his stories written after retirement was the novelette 'In Bad Company', which gave its title to the collection of essays and tales published in 1901. A mixture of facts and fantasy about the strikes of 1890, it is a thoroughgoing condemnation of unionism, a word, he said, 'which really meant rebellion and anarchy' (p. 73). Enthusiastically patriotic, by his own meaning of the term, he had some active interest in the Federal movement and sat on the platform with Deakin and others at a Federation meeting in April 1898[41] but he was disillusioned by the end of 1903, and he wrote to his publisher 'The board will probably be swept at the forthcoming Federal Elections by the labour [sic] candidates—Federation so far has been a failure. We are not ripe for it. We have not the men—so far at least'.[42] The Australian native-born types may be 'stalwart men and wholesome' (*In Bad Company* p. 356), but they should stay in their place, unless by diligence and hard work (or an inheritance) they can rise to join the property owners and governors of the land.

An essential conservatism both of attitude and literary style inevitably meant that the majority of Browne's works had no direct influence on other writers of his own time or later. Almost by accident he wrote one novel, of no great depth, but of much excitement, which captured the flavour of Australian speech, presented a romantic folk-lore figure in familiar surroundings and gave Australian writing its first recognizably and completely Australian types. It is historically important; it is also highly enjoyable reading.

Acknowledgements, Notes and References

Acknowledgement is due to the National Library of Australia, the British Museum, Barr Smith and Mitchell Libraries and the State Library of Victoria for the use of material in their collections, and the willing help of their officers. For permission to use copyright material from *The Stories of Henry Lawson*, edited by Cecil Mann, and *A History of Australian Literature* by H. M. Green, acknowledgement is due to the publishers, Angus & Robertson. I am grateful to the University of Adelaide for financial help and to many people for conversations, especially Mr Hubert Black, T. A. Browne's grandson, who gave generously of his time and allowed me access to family papers.

The general editor has been an appreciated source of guidance and encouragement.

FOOTNOTES

1. T. A. Browne, 'My Autobiography', [*c*. 1906], 32 (Mitchell Library MS., ML Ref. A2132).
2. See W. Scott, *Woodstock* (London, 1901) p. 85.
3. 'My Autobiography', 61-2.
4. Letter of 27 March 1908 in the State Library of Victoria (La Trobe Library Collection, M 5402).
5. *Old Melbourne Memories* (Heinemann, Melbourne, 1969), p. 41. Quotations in the text from Browne's work are in each case from the first one-volume edition except for this book and *Robbery Under Arms* (Oxford University Press, London, 1949).
6. 'The Truth about Aboriginal Outrages', *Life*, III, vi (1906), 544.
7. T. Inglis Moore, *Rolf Boldrewood* (Melbourne, 1968), p. 8.
8. The four quotations from the *Gulgong Guardian* are, respectively, from the issues of 22 May 1871, 8 March 1873, 19 March 1873 and 24 May 1873.
9. K. Burke, 'Gold and Silver, Ch. 5. Thomas Alexander Browne', *Australasian Photo-Review*, LXI, ii (1954), 72-81. See also R. B. Walker, 'History and Fiction in Rolf Boldrewood's *The Miner's Right*', *Australian Literary Studies*, III, i (1967), 28-40.
10. *In Bad Company* (London, 1901), pp. 252-3.
11. Letter in the Mitchell Library (ML Ref. Ab 98/5).
12. See J. Tighe Ryan, 'An Australian Novelist, Rolf Boldrewood', *Review of Reviews*, IV, v (1894), 125-30. The account of writing *Robbery Under Arms* given there differs slightly from that in 'How I Wrote *Robbery Under Arms*', *Life*, I, i (1904), 58-61.

45

13. See J. S. Ryan, 'Rolf Boldrewood in Armidale', *Armidale and District Historical Society Journal and Proceedings*, No. 12 (1969), 86-96.

14. Browne's Diary, 19 April 1904 (Australian National Library MS. 3208).

15. Letter of 25 March 1895 (British Museum Add. MS. 54939, fo. 50).

16. Diary, 4 June 1904.

17. 'Heralds of Australian Literature', *Report of the Fourth Meeting of the Australasian Association for the Advancement of Science* (Sydney, 1893), 808.

18. 'The Silence of Dean Maitland', *Sydney Quarterly Magazine*, V, iii (1888), 215-22.

    'The Stage Australian', *Sydney Quarterly Magazine*, IV, iv (1887), 338-47.

19. '. . . he dates his literary career from the publication of his first and most successful novel, *Robbery Under Arms*, which he did not write until he was sixty-two. He had written only occasional sketches before that' (*Bookman*, XLIII (1912), 89). As well as giving Browne's age when the book was published, instead of when it was written, this brief article, based on a letter from his son, Everard, contains several other extraordinary statements. The most bizarre claims that the Marston boys were modelled on the sons of an employee of Browne, and that 'one of them enlisted, served in South Africa, distinguished himself, won the Victoria Cross and, going home, married a lady of family'.

20. Letter of 21 September 1892 in the British Museum (Add. MS. 54939, fo. 35).

21. Cutting in Diary, 8 April 1898. For further notes on the Becke affair see *Biblionews*, V (1952), iii, 7-8; vii, 21; New Series I (1966), i, 19; ii, 21-2; and A. Grove Day, *Louis Becke* (New York, 1966), pp. 107-10.

22. Diary, 5 December 1898.

23. Diary, 7 May 1904.

24. G. C. Johnson, quoted by Burke, *Australasian Photo-Review*, LXI, ii (1954), 72.

25. *Gulgong Guardian*, 3 June 1871.

26. Counsel for the defendants in the Gulgong case was Dr Belinfante.

27. *Saturday Review*, 29 November 1890, 622.

28. Letter of 22 January 1901 (B.M. Add. MS. 54939, fo. 82v).

29. *Review of Reviews*, IV, v (1894), 129. 'Five Men's Lives for One Horse' appeared first in the *Antipodean*, London, 1893, 8-13, and was collected in *In Bad Company* (1901).

30. *Life*, I, i, (1904), 59. See also R. B. Walker, 'The Historical Basis of *Robbery Under Arms*', *Australian Literary Studies*, II, i (1965), 3-14.

31. See letter of 25 January 19— from Browne's daughter, Mrs Emily Black, to Mrs Alice Hoare, in the Mitchell Library (ML Ref. Ab 98/5). Mrs Black mistakenly gives Longmans as the first publishers.

32. See *Life*, *ibid.*, R. B. Walker, *ibid.*, and *Australian Heritage*, I, xxvii (1970), [iii].

33. The modern German playwright Brecht used the term *verfrumdungeffekt* to describe a means of deliberately calling the audience's attention to the make-believe nature of what they are watching. The cry of a boobook owl occurs as a warning, again unheeded, in Edward Harrington's ballad, 'Morgan', written, however, in the twentieth century. (See *Australian Bush Ballads*, ed. D. Stewart and N. Keesing, Sydney, 1955, p. 35).

34. 'The Bloody Field of Wheogo', Stewart and Keesing, p. 14. The poem appeared in the *Sydney Morning Herald* of 23 August 1862, signed 'Snowy River', and refers to Pottinger's abortive attempt to capture Frank Gardiner a fortnight earlier.

35. For differing views see V. Palmer, *The Legend of the Nineties* (Melbourne, 1966), p. 67, and T. I. Moore, *Rolf Boldrewood* (Melbourne, 1968), p. 24. Examples of repentance ballads can be found in such collections as *The Shirburn Ballads* (Oxford, 1907); and for a bushranging ballad with a warning see 'The Death of Morgan', Stewart and Keesing, pp. 34-5.

36. Rolf Boldrewood, 'How I Wrote *Robbery Under Arms*', *Life*, I, i (1904), 61.

37. See K. Burke, *Thomas Alexander Browne: an annotated bibliography, checklist and chronology* (Cremorne, 1956), pp. 57-8; Cecil Mann, ed., *The Stories of Henry Lawson*, First Series (Sydney, 1964), p. 25; *Life*, I, i (1904), 59.

38. *Saturday Review*, 25 August 1888, 244.

39. Nettie Palmer, *Modern Australian Literature* (Melbourne, 1924), p. 6; H. M. Green, *A History of Australian Literature* (Sydney, 1961), i, 225.

40. See C. Hartley Grattan, ed., *Australia* (Berkeley, 1947), p. 293; Thomas Wood, introd., *Robbery Under Arms* (London, 1949), p. xiii; C. Hamer, 'Boldrewood Reassessed', *Southerly*, XXVI, iv (1966), 263-78; R. B. Walker, *op cit.*; also Frank Sargeson, review of *Robbery Under Arms*, *Landfall*, IV, iii, 1950, 262-5; and Alan Brissenden, introd., *Robbery Under Arms* (Penrith, 1968).

41. Diary, 5 April 1898.

42. B.M. Add. MS. 54939, fo. 99.

47

Bibliography

WORKS OF BOLDREWOOD

Fiction

'The Fencing of Wanderowna'. *Australian Town and Country Journal*, 7 June-23 August 1873. [Included in *A Romance of Canvas Town* (see below).]

'Incidents and Adventures of My Run Home'. *Australian Town and Country Journal*, 10 January-19 December 1874. As *My Run Home*. Macmillan, London, 1897.

'The Squatter's Dream'. *Australian Town and Country Journal*, 23 January-27 November 1875. As *Ups and Downs*. S. W. Silver & Co., London, 1878. As *The Squatter's Dream*. Macmillan, London, 1890.

'A Colonial Reformer'. *Australian Town and Country Journal*, 1 July 1876-23 June 1877. As book. Macmillan, London, 1890.

'The Wild Australian'. *Australian Town and Country Journal*, 30 June-29 September 1877.

'An Australian Squire'. *Australian Town and Country Journal*, 6 October 1877-1 February 1879. As *Babes in the Bush*. Macmillan, London, 1900.

'The Miner's Right'. *Australian Town and Country Journal*, 3 January-18 December 1880. *The Colonies and India* (London), 21 February 1880-12 March 1881. As book. Macmillan, London, 1890.

'Robbery Under Arms'. *Sydney Mail*, 1 July 1882-11 August 1883. As book. Remington, London, 1888. [Later editions include those introduced by Charles Barrett (Cassell, London, 1947); Thomas Wood (World's Classics, Oxford University Press, London, 1949); Alan Brissenden (Discovery Press, Penrith, 1968); and R. B. Walker (Macmillan, Melbourne, 1968).]

'The Sealskin Mantle'. *Sydney Mail*, 16 February 1884-7 February 1885. As *The Sealskin Cloak*. Macmillan, London, 1896.

'The Final Choice: or Pollie's Probation'. *Australasian*, 19 December 1885 (Christmas Supplement). As *The Crooked Stick*. Macmillan, London, 1895.

'A Sydney-Side Saxon'. *Centennial Magazine*, September 1888-January 1889. As book. Macmillan, London, 1891.

'Nevermore'. *Centennial Magazine*, August 1889-September 1890. As book. Macmillan, London, 1892.

A Modern Buccaneer. Macmillan, London, 1894.

The Sphinx of Eaglehawk. Macmillan, London, 1895.

Plain Living. Macmillan, London, 1898.

A Romance of Canvas Town and Other Stories. Macmillan, London, 1898.

War to the Knife, or Tangata Maori. Macmillan, London, 1899.

In Bad Company and Other Stories. Macmillan, London, 1901.

The Ghost Camp or The Avengers. Macmillan, London, 1902.

The Last Chance. Macmillan, London, 1905.

Non-Fiction

S. W. Silver & Co.'s Australian Grazier's Guide. London, 1879. [Anon.]

S. W. Silver & Co.'s Australian Grazier's Guide No. II—Cattle. London, 1881. [Anon.]

Old Melbourne Memories. G. Robertson, Melbourne, 1884. [New edition with introduction and notes by C. E. Sayers. Heinemann, Melbourne, 1969.]

'Heralds of Australian Literature'. *Report of the Fourth Meeting of the Australasian Association for the Advancement of Science.* Sydney, 1893, pp. 799-811.

Selected Biography and Criticism

Burke, Keast. *Thomas Alexander Browne (Rolf Boldrewood): an annotated bibliography, checklist and chronology.* Stone Copying Co., Cremorne, 1956.

Byrne, Desmond. *Australian Writers.* Bentley, London, 1896.

Green, H. M. *A History of Australian Literature.* Angus & Robertson, Sydney, 1961.

Hamer, C. 'Boldrewood Reassessed'. *Southerly,* XXVI (1966), 263-78.

Mares, F. H. 'Henry Kingsley, Marcus Clarke and Rolf Boldrewood', in Dutton, Geoffrey (ed.), *The Literature of Australia.* Penguin, Melbourne, 1964.

Miller, E. Morris. *Australian Literature.* Melbourne University Press, Melbourne, 1940.

Moore, T. Inglis. *Rolf Boldrewood.* Oxford University Press, Melbourne, 1968. (Great Australians series.)

Australian Dictionary of Biography vol. 3. Melbourne University Press, Melbourne, 1969, pp. 267-9.

Walker, R. B. 'The Historical Basis of *Robbery Under Arms*'. *Australian Literary Studies,* II, i (1965), 3-14. [Repeated substantially in Walker's edition, see above.]

'History and Fiction in Rolf Boldrewood's *The Miner's Right*', *Australian Literary Studies,* III, i (1967), 28-40.

AUSTRALIAN WRITERS AND THEIR WORK

BARCROFT BOAKE – *Clement Semmler*
ROLF BOLDREWOOD – *Alan Brissenden*
MARTIN BOYD – *Kathleen Fitzpatrick*
CHRISTOPHER BRENNAN – *James McAuley*
JOHN LE GAY BRERETON – *H. P. Heseltine*
FRANK DALBY DAVISON – *Hume Dow*
EARLY AUSTRALIAN CHILDREN'S LITERATURE – *Rosemary Wighton*
MILES FRANKLIN – *Ray Mathew*
JOSEPH FURPHY – *John Barnes*
ADAM LINDSAY GORDON – *W. H. Wilde*
CHARLES HARPUR – *Judith Wright*
WILLIAM GOSSE HAY – *Fayette Gosse*
HENRY KINGSLEY AND COLONIAL FICTION – *John Barnes*
NORMAN LINDSAY – *John Hetherington*
KENNETH MACKENZIE – *Evan Jones*
JAMES MCAULEY – *Vivian Smith*
JOHN SHAW NEILSON – *H. J. Oliver*
A. B. PATERSON – *Clement Semmler*
VANCE PALMER – *Vivian Smith*
KATHERINE SUSANNAH PRICHARD – *Henrietta Drake-Brockman*
HENRY HANDEL RICHARDSON – *Vincent Buckley*
CHRISTINA STEAD – *R. G. Geering*
DOUGLAS STEWART – *Nancy Keesing*
LOUIS STONE – *H. J. Oliver*
THREE RADICALS – *W. H. Wilde*
PATRICK WHITE – *Geoffrey Dutton*

In Preparation:

CHRISTOPHER BRENNAN (new edition) – *James McAuley*
CRITICISM – *Brian Kiernan*
DRAMA – *Margaret Williams*
XAVIER HERBERT – *H. P. Heseltine*
HAL PORTER – *Mary Lord*

[Continued overleaf

To Come:

MARTIN BOYD (new edition) – *Brenda Niall*
MARCUS CLARKE – *Michael Wilding*
R. D. FITZGERALD – *G. A. Wilkes*
JOSEPH FURPHY (new edition) – *John Barnes*
A. D. HOPE – *Leonie Kramer*
HENRY KENDALL – *T. L. Sturm*
HENRY LAWSON (new edition) – *Stephen Murray-Smith*
RECENT FICTION – *R. G. Geering*
KENNETH SLESSOR – *Graham Burns*
A. G. STEPHENS – *W. M. Maidment*
THREE WOMEN NOVELISTS – *Cecil Hadgraft & Ray Beilby*
JUDITH WRIGHT – *A. D. Hope*

Bibliography:

AUSTRALIAN WRITING: A SELECT BIBLIOGRAPHY – *Grahame Johnston*